"Christians the world over pray as Jesus taught them, saying, 'Thy will be done on earth as it is in heaven.' Michael Allen digs up new treasures from this phrase, arguing that heavenly hope—for eternal life in fellowship with the triune God—ought to inform our earthly way of life. The four chapters in this book work variations on the theme that the norms for Christian behavior today (ethics) are related to our hope for tomorrow (eschatology). Contra Marx, it turns out that heaven is not the opiate of the people, lulling them into indifference to present injustices, but a potent stimulant to work for the good of others, denying oneself and, in the process, communicating God's goodness and displaying God's coming kingdom. Allen's call to heavenly-mindedness on earth is a provocative corrective to the contemporary emphasis on earth-bound conceptions of heaven."

— KEVIN J. VANHOOZER
Trinity Evangelical Divinity School

"Can we still say, with the disciple Philip, 'Lord, show us the Father, and we shall be satisfied' (John 14:8)? Is the desire of our hearts ordered to everlasting communion with the Holy Trinity, so that eternal life will rejoice us insofar as we share in Life? Instructed preeminently by John Calvin and John Owen, Michael Allen urges that our encounter with Jesus Christ's eschatological words and deeds must give us the spiritual-mindedness and self-denial that configure us (and this world) to the Lord whom we love. Ecumenical readers will find this book to be, at its core, an exercise in sound biblical and Augustinian good sense."

— MATTHEW LEVERING
Mundelein Seminary

"With his characteristic clarity and verve, Michael Allen presents an alternative to the recent evangelical trend of thinning down heaven to human—all too human—proportions. In its place, Allen articulates a richly theocentric account of heaven that affixes our affections and actions to the proper end of creation and redemption—the triune God made known in Jesus Christ. In the process, he presents an astonishingly counter-cultural vision of the Christian life lived in a 'heavenly-minded' manner. This lively book is a conversation-changer!"

— J. TODD BILLINGS
Western Theological Seminary

"In this provocative book Michael Allen reorients our thinking and our lives by, as he says, challenging us to 'recenter' our Christian hope and life on God himself. We need Allen's voice in this conversation, for his arguments are not simply about the future, but about how we live in the present, helping us make sense of the biblical call of self-denial and heavenly-mindedness as we long to be with Christ."

— KELLY M. KAPIC
Covenant College

"This is a splendid volume. Drawing deeply from the past while engaging a wide variety of contemporary voices, Michael Allen nevertheless summarizes the richness of Reformed teaching with clarity and insight. His *Grounded in Heaven* focuses on the main issues, and beneath its superb brevity lies a deep reservoir of research."

— MICHAEL HORTON
Westminster Seminary California

Grounded in Heaven

Recentering Christian Hope and Life on God

Michael Allen

WILLIAM B. EERDMANS PUBLISHING COMPANY
GRAND RAPIDS, MICHIGAN

Wm. B. Eerdmans Publishing Co.
4035 Park East Court SE, Grand Rapids, Michigan 49546
www.eerdmans.com

27 26 25 24   7 8 9 10

ISBN 978-0-8028-7453-5

Library of Congress Cataloging-in-Publication Data

Names: Allen, Michael, 1981– author.
Title: Grounded in heaven : recentering Christian hope and life on God /
    Michael Allen.
Description: Grand Rapids : Eerdmans Publishing Co., 2018. |
    Includes bibliographical references and index.
Identifiers: LCCN 2018035457 | ISBN 9780802874535 (pbk. : alk. paper)
Subjects: LCSH: Desire for God. | Beatific vision. | Spiritual life—Christianity. |
    Hope—Religious aspects—Christianity.
Classification: LCC BV4817 .A45 2018 | DDC 231.7—dc23
    LC record available at https://lccn.loc.gov/2018035457

For the generous supporters of Reformed Theological Seminary,

partners in the gospel and models of living hope.

CONTENTS

ACKNOWLEDGMENTS

Self-denial begins with acknowledging others, not only the God in whom we live, move, and have our being, but also those brothers and sisters through whom we are sustained and strengthened. In preparing this book, many have blessed me and given needed help.

Reformed Theological Seminary has offered support of various sorts. The Board of Trustees, Ligon Duncan, and Scott Swain have encouraged me to write and given me the time and space to do so. Our librarian, Michael Farrell, has patiently chased down resources for me time and again. My students have interacted with more texts in patristic and Puritan ascetical theology than perhaps they expected when moving to the Magic Kingdom of central Florida, and those classroom discussions have provided creative ferment for my own writing.

Some material in this book has been published elsewhere. Chapter 2 was previously released in Brill's *Journal of Reformed Theology*, and a version of chapter 4 appeared in a *Festschrift* volume published by Mohr Siebeck. I thank both publishers for permission to reproduce that work here. I also explored the various topics here in a five-part series on theological eschatology commissioned by Mark McDowell for the Reformation21 blog.

Feedback from readers there helped encourage and clarify what I wanted to say in the book form.

A number of friends and colleagues have patiently read and commented upon the manuscript. Todd Billings, Hans Boersma, Wesley Hill, Matthew Levering, Scott Swain, and Geoff Ziegler were generous with their time and advice. The late John Webster offered some significant comments on the first three chapters. Members of the faculty colloquium at Reformed Theological Seminary and the neighboring Reformation Bible College offered feedback on the first chapter in early 2015. Finally, James Ernest has helped me bring the manuscript to its final form. I am delighted to have worked with him and the team at Eerdmans on this project.

Family and friends have walked with me in times of trial and difficulty and consistently reminded me of my heavenly hope. My wife Emily has cared for me amidst physical challenges and always offered her love as a testament to a hope greater than mere bodily health. My extended family and my sons have modeled prayer and patience (and not a little self-sacrifice) amidst earthly trials. Our congregation, New City PCA in Orlando, and our pastor, Damein Schitter, have modeled attentiveness unto the living Lord whose grace is never extinguished. This book was prepared amidst some of the most challenging days of my life, but it was not undertaken alone. Phil Letizia, Wesley Hill, Scott Swain, Ryan Peterson, and Ronnie Perry stand out for their prayer and encouragement.

I dedicate this volume to the many saints who long for the city that is to come and selflessly sacrifice their earthly treasures to raise up and equip those who will lead congregations in years to come and in places all around the globe. Their lives of loving generosity model a resolute and vibrant hope in Christ and his kingdom. To the supporters of Reformed Theological Seminary, I offer this book with gratitude and much hope.

The Eclipse of Heaven

Sometimes you can see a trend by noting the exception.

In his well-regarded book *How (Not) to Be Secular*, the philosopher James K. A. Smith observes that the Reformation's celebration of the theological significance of the ordinary not only served as a remarkable element of lay renewal in Christianity but also was "the camel's nose in the tent of enchantment—that somehow the Protestant Reformation opened the door to what would become, by a winding, contingent path, exclusive humanism."[1] Throughout that book, Smith not only offers a brief and accessible genealogy for this trend toward an exclusive humanism but also prompts his readers to consider the need to think beyond the "immanent frame" and to keep in mind higher or greater ends.

Smith's diagnosis is stark as he speaks of an "eclipse of heaven" and a focus upon ends that are material and earthy, not spiritual or transcendent. Notice that, in so doing, he does not merely address ills outside the church, or even maladies marking the revisionist churches or the skeptical or nominal Christian, in ecclesiastical or sociological terms. Rather, he says: "So even our theism becomes humanized, immanentized, and the *telos* of God's

1. James K. A. Smith, *How (Not) to Be Secular: Reading Charles Taylor* (Grand Rapids: Eerdmans, 2014), 39.

providential concern is circumscribed within immanence. And this becomes true even of 'orthodox' folk: 'even people who held to orthodox beliefs were influenced by this humanizing trend; frequently the transcendent dimension of their faith became less central.' Because eternity is eclipsed, the this-worldly is amplified and threatens to swallow all."[2]

As mentioned above, a trend can be seen by observing the exception. Smith, a professor at Calvin College, a leading institution in the neo-Calvinist or Kuyperian world, has addressed a naturalizing tendency and has pointed again to the need to have hopes beyond the mundane and the material. That is no small thing. Ever since Kuyper articulated the significance of all things—all spheres, all facets of life for one's vocation before Christ—the churches, the institutions, and the social world influenced by neo-Calvinist thought have focused their significant intellectual vitality heavily (and, regularly, with very sharp polemics) against spiritualism and for creation, materiality, sociality, and all things humane. To see a leading light in the Kuyperian world then speaking up for heaven is a significant matter.

It is also no small thing that this emphasis arose in this particular book by Smith, for *How (Not) to Be Secular* is a volume subtitled *Reading Charles Taylor*. Smith here performs yeoman's work in accessibly and thoughtfully conveying many of the intellectual analyses provided in the work of the Roman Catholic philosopher, in particular those found in his *A Secular Age* (a tome that, like his earlier *Sources of the Self*, is both profound and also inaccessible to many ordinary readers). In previous works, Smith has not emphasized this kind of spiritual transcendence with anything like the regularity found in *How (Not) to Be Secular*. Footnotes suggest that the input of Hans Boersma's book *Heavenly Participation* (released only in 2011) may have played a formative role there.[3] But

---

2. Smith, *How (Not) to Be Secular*, 49–50.
3. Hans Boersma, *Heavenly Participation: The Weaving of a Sacramen-*

it seems obvious and straightforward to note that a Roman Catholic has suggested the significance of what those participating in parallel discussions in the neo-Calvinist world have not addressed on their own.

On Eschatological Naturalism

A variety of authors in recent years have sought to draw Christians away from the dangers of segmenting their lives. The maladies can be described under varying terminology: sometimes "Gnosticism" is the label for such dualistic divisions of our lives; sometimes "Platonism" or "Platonizing" serves as the moniker for this mishap whereby we seek flight from our context; sometimes "spiritualism" depicts a malformed view of God's involvement with his creatures, as if the triune God only interacted with us in certain liturgical or religious moments and nowhere else.

These polemical concerns have been voiced in academic and popular forms. N. T. Wright has asked, "First, what is the ultimate Christian hope? Second, what hope is there for change, rescue, transformation, new possibilities within the world in the present?" He has warned that "as long as we see Christian hope in terms of 'going to heaven,' of a salvation that is essentially away from this world, the two questions are bound to appear as unrelated."[4] He consistently warns against Platonizing, rarely, if ever,

---

tal Tapestry (Grand Rapids: Eerdmans, 2011). For other recent reflections on the need to recover a spiritual final end, see also Matthew Levering, *Jesus and the Demise of Death: Resurrection, Afterlife, and the Fate of the Christian* (Waco, TX: Baylor University Press, 2012); Isaac Augustine Morales, "'With My Body I Thee Worship': New Creation, Beatific Vision, and the Liturgical Consummation of All Things," *Pro Ecclesia* 25, no. 3 (2016): 337–56; and especially Charles T. Matthewes, *A Theology of Public Life*, Cambridge Studies in Christian Doctrine (Cambridge: Cambridge University Press, 2008).

4. N. T. Wright, *Surprised by Hope: Rethinking Heaven, the Resurrection, and the Mission of the Church* (New York: HarperOne, 2008), 5.

defining and substantiating such worries. Far more common is a quip such as, "What about the blatant Platonism of the hymn 'Abide with Me,' still a favorite in some circles? 'Heaven's morning breaks, and earth's vain shadows flee.'"[5] The line is neither anti-earthly nor Platonic in any way, but it does speak of the sun's rays breaking in upon and illumining earth, dispelling the night wherein earth is bereft of the sun's full light. That a statement is made about earth being needy apart from heaven does not a Platonism make, much less a fault show.

Many helpful words are found in Wright's treatise and in similar books. He calls for Christmas to be read with Easter, not apart from it.[6] He warns about the kind of cultural tumult that has led to a normalizing of cremation instead of burial, suggesting that it bespeaks a lack of respect for the embodied state.[7] He pulls together strong arguments regarding the truth of the Easter claim.[8] These and other discrete points are spot-on. And his overall concern to wed eschatology and ethics rides with the course of prophetic and then apostolic exhortation.[9] Yet his argument consistently tacks toward the earthly and minimizes or mocks the heavenly, the beatific, the liturgical, and especially anything that he might deem Platonic.

Wright's focus on how God creates space for others, specifically for earthly and embodied others, in our future hope has had widespread effect. Wright drew the rabbinical notion of *zimzum* back into eschatological discussion, suggesting (contra Jürgen Moltmann) that God makes new space in the future for others. More recently, Rob Bell has advanced this notion at great length

---

5. Wright, *Surprised by Hope*, 21.
6. Wright, *Surprised by Hope*, 23.
7. Wright, *Surprised by Hope*, 24.
8. Wright, *Surprised by Hope*, 53–76.
9. See especially Wright, *Surprised by Hope*, 207–32 (where he addresses present concern for justice, beauty, and evangelism in light of the Christian hope).

in his book *The Zimzum of Love*, and for some time he has advocated (in terms similar to Wright) a concern for how our hope is viewed.[10] For Bell and others, justice and beauty are as significant as evangelism; for them, embodiment and earthly harmony or shalom mark the center of our future hope.[11] Whether in the more academic arguments of Wright or the theological haiku of Bell, however, we see that the turn to the embodied, political, and earthly has tended to eclipse heaven. Getting underneath and exploring this shift demands that we dig further back to see from where such movements have come, and so we must explore the widespread influence and popularizing of the neo-Calvinist tradition regarding Christian eschatology.

Abraham Kuyper famously declared a century ago that there is not one square inch upon this earth of which Jesus Christ does not say "Mine!" We might expand, as he and his followers have done so, by paraphrasing that there is not one nook or cranny of human existence over which Christ does not claim lordship. This insistence on the sovereignty of Christ in all things and in all areas of life has prompted development of worldview thinking and has underwritten numerous educational initiatives in the twentieth and now twenty-first centuries, not only within the Dutch Reformed community (in places like Calvin College) but also well outside that ethnic and ecclesiastical world (as evidenced by the way in which Arthur Holmes and Wheaton College would famously describe their educational and missional commitments with language that "all truth is God's truth" or "the integration of faith and learning").

The vitality of Kuyperianism has been that centrifugal energy whereby classic Christian and even Reformed theology has been applied to new disciplines and arenas of life. A principled

10. Rob Bell and Kristen Bell, *The Zimzum of Love* (New York: Harper-One, 2016).

11. See also "the future question" addressed by Brian McLaren, *A New Kind of Christianity: Ten Questions That Are Transforming the Faith* (New York: HarperOne, 2011), 191–206.

ethics has been articulated across the board; I say this ethics or this sense of calling is principled because it flows from fundamental commitments about the gospel and, more widely, about biblical teaching regarding humanity: our nature and our ends. Specifically, Kuyperianism in its various iterations has emphasized our creation as holistic beings—embodied, social, intellectual—and our destiny as not only redeemed but even restored sons and daughters of the Most High—resurrected, at peace with one another, wise, etc. A particular eschatology has marked this strain of theological and ethical development.

Surely the greatest theologian of the neo-Calvinist tradition is Herman Bavinck. His four-volume *Reformed Dogmatics* continues to have the most sizable impact of any text from that tradition, at least in the realm of doctrine. One of the great traits of Bavinck's work, across its wide terrain, is its evenhandedness in judgment: the theological master had a keen sense of balance, proportionality, and, thus, did not tend to overreact to one thing by falling too far elsewhere. While maintaining Protestant and Reformed distinctives not only with vigor but also with an uncommon clarity, Bavinck manages to glean more from sources traditionally engaged only by Roman Catholics in the late nineteenth- and early twentieth-century context (e.g., the Thomist tradition of reflection on nature and grace). Interestingly, however, Bavinck's eschatology, which forms the culmination of his fourth volume, focuses not only narrowly but also polemically upon the notion of the new creation over against more spiritual emphases found elsewhere in the Christian tradition. A controversial concern (some sort of escapist hope that has little or nothing to do with human existence here) seems to mark his reflections in an uncharacteristic manner.[12]

12. The naturalistic tilt of much neo-Calvinist eschatology does not seem to arise from Abraham Kuyper's own eschatology, which maintained a vibrant mystical and theocentric impulse. Hans Boersma's essay "Blessing and Glory: Abraham Kuyper on the Beatific Vision," *Calvin Theological Journal*

In recent years neo-Calvinists (such as Richard Middleton) and those influenced by that tradition (such as N. T. Wright, strongly influenced by Brian Walsh) have spoken in even sharper terms regarding the earthy nature of the Christian hope. Richard Middleton's recent book *A New Heaven and a New Earth* is subtitled *Reclaiming Biblical Eschatology*. Clearly it suggests that a biblical vision of our hope has been lost, and it identifies the problematic early on when speaking of "the problem of otherworldly hope."[13] Middleton says heaven is not our destiny and speaks of popular songs or expressions of piety that suggest such concepts as being "lies."[14] Middleton not only says next to nothing about the spiritual or heavenly reality of our hope but he critiques or openly mocks those who do. The famous quip may say that "hope springs eternal," but this current of recent Reformed eschatology surely has not sprinted in that direction.

I find the term "eschatological naturalism" useful to depict this tendency within the neo-Calvinist tradition, though I mean the term "naturalism" only in a very specific manner. With regard to the *telos* or end of our hope, a significant strand of modern theology (influenced by the worldview of Kuyper) has articulated that hope in a naturalistic or materialistic manner. Charles Taylor and James K. A. Smith have noted this as well, so I am not venturing a thesis alone. I do think it is worth reflecting on how strange it is, though, that this immanentism would settle in to the conservative or traditional Reformed world. These are Augustinians who believe

---

52 (2017): 205–41, as well as the book of which it is a part (*Seeing God: The Beatific Vision in Christian Tradition* [Grand Rapids: Eerdmans, 2018]), will be a helpful resource in this regard.

13. J. Richard Middleton, *A New Heaven and a New Earth: Reclaiming Biblical Eschatology* (Grand Rapids: Baker Academic, 2015), 21–34. See similar moves made in Wright, *Surprised by Hope*, and Michael Wittmer, *Heaven Is a Place on Earth: Why Everything You Do Matters to God* (Grand Rapids: Zondervan, 2004).

14. Middleton, *A New Heaven and a New Earth*, 236–37 and 27, respectively.

in divine sovereignty and effective divine agency behind not just Christian salvation but all human history, providentially speaking. They have as wide and deep a notion of divine presence throughout our world and generations as exists in the Christian world. But when it comes to the climax of redemptive history, neo-Calvinists have often turned from focus upon communion with Christ, the presence of God, or the beatific vision (the classical image for the eschatological spiritual presence of the Almighty) to focus instead upon the resurrected body, the shalom of the city, and the renewal of the earth. Naturalism is no surprise in modernity, as Taylor explains, but eschatological naturalism ought to be a shock.

Toward a Systematic Theology of Evangelical Hope

Alert to Taylor's assessment and mindful of Smith's prompt, to this trend toward what I'm calling "eschatological naturalism," then, I offer a series of reflections here regarding how we might consider the Christian hope in a way that does acknowledge the breadth of Reformational and even neo-Calvinist reflection without losing sight of the spiritual center of that hope in life with God. I do so as one who identifies with the neo-Calvinist movement autobiographically and theologically. I went to a Christian high school in Miami where baseball may have been marked by Alex Rodriguez, but the philosophy of education was shaped by its Dutch Reformed and Kuyperian heritage. I benefitted from a systemic model of Christian education at Wheaton College, where its liberal arts model and theological identity have been influenced over the past century in numerous ways by the neo-Calvinist world. And, as a seminary professor, I have assigned Herman Bavinck's *Reformed Dogmatics* as much as any other single text written in the modern age.

I do think, however, that the neo-Calvinist emphases upon the new creation and the earthiness of our hope can and have morphed at times from being productive Reformed corrections to the catholic faith to being parasitic to the basic lineaments of the Christian gospel. Too often a desire to value the ordinary and the everyday, the mundane and the material, has not led to what ought to be common sense to any Bible-reader: that heaven and the spiritual realm matter most highly. Too rarely do we speak of heavenly-mindedness, spiritual-mindedness, self-denial, or any of the terminology that has marked the ascetical tradition (in its patristic or, later, in its Reformed iterations).

In the chapters that follow, I will not be sketching an entire eschatology, of course, but I will be seeking to outline some fundamental moves that would shape such a project. This book is an infusion of certain eschatological and ethical nutrients, seeking to make up for a serious deficiency, and it should not be taken as a holistic diet for Christian faith and practice. I will attempt to gesture at four moves that are methodologically significant: honoring the priorities of the Bible, thinking across categories or doctrines to pursue an integrative and coherent theology, attending to the breadth and diversity of biblical teachings, and, finally, observing the way in which action or ethical behavior is always drawn from scriptural description of reality. In each methodological maneuver, I will try to note how a particular material feature of biblical eschatology comes to light, presenting the basic structures of an evangelical hope that is centered upon the covenant presence of God, calibrating that presence in a Christ-centered way, highlighting the way in which that hope is one that shapes our living by focusing our attention upon heaven. Finally, I will tease out how the same Jesus who has already justified us now calls us through his prophetic and apostolic emissaries to die and to sacrifice for the sake of a greater hope and life (thus reclaiming a distinctly evangelical asceticism, in the tradition of Calvin and the Puritans and their reception of the patristic ascetical tradition).

Some orientation ought to be given to the reader before we launch into the argument. First, we ought to explain why eschatology and ethics do well to be thought of together. Though biblical scholars have drawn out this connection in recent decades, it still remains underappreciated. Though we cannot draw the entirety of our ethics out of eschatological teaching (for we must also root moral theology in creation and other facets of Christian teaching), we cannot understand the moral summons of the triune God apart from the ends unto which he beckons his daughters and sons. Second, we must face head-on the biggest charge against my interjection, namely, that it would lead to a moral quietism. Indeed, some might suggest that a heavenly-mindedness is the preserve of the privileged and a luxury that cannot be enjoyed by the precious brothers and sisters suffering in various ways around the globe. If true, it would show the incompatibility of my project with the ways of Jesus and the God of Israel, for they plainly show a propensity to draw close to the marginalized. Yet I believe we can see that a heavenly-mindedness and an approach that is genuinely attentive to the priority (though not exclusivity) of the spiritual and theological will actually deepen and further an alertness and activism regarding matters of loving our neighbor, the excluded "Other," and even our enemies. Finally, we ought to comment on the structure of the book and the way in which it argues for theological retrieval as well as evangelical reform, seeking to model a full-orbed dogmatic account by engaging the catholic tradition and yet moving forward in a Reformed key.

Living Hope: On the Connection of Eschatology and Ethics

The biblical description of discipleship begins at the end of the story. God motivates and summons self-denial and love of neighbor by speaking first of what we are made for and what God gives unto us in Jesus Christ. Future blessing prompts present behavior. The rhythm of the parables of the kingdom of God displays this ethical logic time after time. When we assess the worth, beauty, and goodness of the treasure hid in the field, then and only then do we joyfully sell all we have to buy that field (Matt 13:44).

The apostolic writings caught this eschatological ethic and extended it into various situations.[15] The New Testament writings followed Jesus in calling women and men to love their neighbors in radical ways and to deny their own cause for the sake of honoring Christ and blessing others. Romans 12–15 illustrates this kind of moral calling, wherein enemies are to be loved (12:14–21), tyrants are to be honored (13:1–7), and others are to be welcomed (14:1–23). We do well to ask not only what Paul asks of us, but also how he motivates such love. The apostle Paul did not simply speak of justification by faith alone and then summon Roman Christians to moral transformation. Such a sketch would miss the thick depiction of the gospel offered especially in Romans 5–11 and suggest a jump from Romans 4 straight to chapter 12. Paul first attests the brilliant hope we possess as adopted children (ch. 8) and as a people (chs. 9–11). A vivid portrayal of our hope serves to display the "mercies of God" that compel our worship of God through "presenting ourselves as living sacrifices" (Rom 12:1).

Paul suggests in the broadest of terms that hope motivates living in a Christian way. The specific summons outlined in those chapters is consistently depicted as flowing from faith in the specific promise of God.[16] So the radical love of our enemy not only

15. For a number of pastoral meditations in this regard, see Benjamin J. Gladd and Matthew S. Harmon, *Making All Things New: Inaugurated Eschatology for the Life of the Church* (Grand Rapids: Baker Academic, 2016); for a more detailed exegetical sketch of these connections, see G. K. Beale, *A New Testament Biblical Theology: The Unfolding of the Old Testament in the New* (Grand Rapids: Baker Academic, 2011).

16. Romans calls for the "obedience of faith" (Rom 1:5; 16:26), castigates Israel of old for failing to follow the law "by faith" but instead pursuing it "as if it were by works" (9:30–32), and observes that anything done apart from faith is sin (14:23). Like Hebrews 11:1–12:2, then, Romans calls us to obey God and love him and others out of a particular Christian moti-

draws upon Jesus's teaching in the past (Matt 5:42–47) but also looks forward to his promised judgment in the future. Because we know God says "Vengeance is mine; I will repay," we are freed from vigilante-like responses to mistreatment and freed for denying our own rights for the sake of loving others (Rom 12:19). Our created desire for justice and wholeness prompts a yearning for reaction to harm; Paul does not denigrate this desire, though he does redirect it. Paul points us to God's promise that he will right all wrongs in the end, so that we are freed from our hackneyed and invariably inhumane efforts to do so ourselves and freed for the remarkable witness of loving our enemies even as Christ loved us when we were his enemies. Faith prompts works. Hope for what God has promised tomorrow shapes life today.

Spirituality and the Social Status Quo: Isn't Heavenly-Mindedness the Privilege of the Elite?

We might ask, however, if a heavenly minded posture isn't simply the privilege of those with the space and resources to avoid worry about health, provision, and safety. Isn't it remarkably counterproductive to call for deeper heavenly-mindedness when dealing with situations of want, oppression, trauma, or even abuse? Isn't a celestial calling an opiate for the masses or a distraction from real issues worthy of concern? Does this perpetuate abuse or distract from real moral and social reform? Hopefully every Christian deems such challenges worthy of concern, for the social conscience is a gift of God and a sign of being blessed by conformity unto the character of the one who bears the burdens of the weak and runs speedily to the rescue of the downtrodden.[17]

---

vation: faith in the promises of the gospel. Hope draws out a life of worship and witness.

17. See especially the Beatitudes in Matthew 5:3–12 for the way in which moral conformity unto God is part of our blessedness by his grace. Concern

It is worth reading the Bible not only to see what it says regarding certain matters addressed therein but also to observe where and when topics are broached. Heavenly-mindedness does not appear as the luxury of the landed or the privilege of the possessors. In the Bible, a resolute focus upon the future inflections of gospel hope seem to appear in precisely those moments when God's people suffer the deepest pangs of hurt. It is when they have been scattered far from home as "elect exiles of the dispersion" (1 Pet 1:1) and face not only trials of the day (1:6) but also the threat of mistreatment (2:19; 3:6) or persecution (3:14–17) that the apostle Peter addresses the blessed "living hope" brought "through the resurrection of Jesus Christ from the dead," which is "an inheritance that is imperishable, undefiled, and unfading, kept in heaven for you" (1:3–4). The calling to "be self-controlled and sober-minded" and to "keep loving one another earnestly" flows from the pledge that "the end of all things is at hand" (4:2). Peter calls our attention heavenward precisely amidst the present moment pregnant with danger and pain.

The Epistle to the Hebrews similarly orients the imagination of the Christian in a heavenward manner amidst what can only be called a situation of trauma and struggle. The author speaks of struggles the readers have experienced in the past: "But recall the former days when, after you were enlightened, you endured a hard struggle with sufferings, sometimes being publicly exposed to reproach and affliction, and sometimes being partners

---

for moral righteousness and social justice demands biblical and theological definition which cannot simply be taken for granted in a pluralistic society (or, for that matter, in any conversation conducted by sinners like ourselves), but such pangs of conscience also cannot be shirked as if they were optional to the Christoformity promised in the gospel (e.g., Romans 8:29–30 promises that we are predestined to be conformed to the image of God's own Son, the very one who cares and dies even for his enemy). While the activistic objection to a spiritual focus can and should be overcome (see further), it is not wrong for caring deeply about the moral and political implications of God's lordship for all of our behavior.

with those so treated" (10:32–33). It seems as though some were mistreated publicly—likely through imprisonment or other such civic penalties—and others were willing to be identified with those being punished for their faith, quite likely by providing material support for the imprisoned. It seems that this experience of struggle has called into question the very claims of Jesus; if pain and hurt follow, is this a sign that we were wrong to leave the broader Jewish path and follow this purported Messiah?[18] The Hebrews are struggling to continue the journey, and the danger is that they might fall away or give up on Christ altogether by returning to offer temple sacrifices for sin (see 2:1–4; 3:1–4:13; 5:11–6:12; 10:19–39; 12:12–29).

The motivation unto continued faithfulness offered again and again in Hebrews takes a number of forms, one of which is heavenly. Indeed, Hebrews 10 draws out this angle in speaking to the fact that the readers have not yet apostasized amidst suffering. "For you had compassion on those in prison, and you joyfully accepted the plundering of your property, since you knew that you yourselves had a better possession and an abiding one" (10:34). The "better possession," which alone is "abiding," has given comfort to their waylaid souls. And they have not made shipwreck of their faith. This congregation shares a "heavenly calling" (3:1), and they share this end with saints of years past whose stories are recounted in chapter 11.

Struggle is not rare but regular in this litany of the faithful, and again the celestial characterizes the motivating impulse of these bygone women and men.

> These all died in faith, not having received the things
> promised, but having seen them and greeted them from
> afar, and having acknowledged that they were strangers
> and exiles on the earth. For people who speak thus make

18. John the Baptist expressed a similar concern in Matthew 11:2–6.

it clear that they are seeking a homeland. If they had been thinking of that land from which they had gone out, they would have had opportunity to return. But as it is, they desire a better country, that is, a heavenly one. Therefore God is not ashamed to be called their God, for he has prepared for them a city. (11:13–16)

Like the "better possession" spoken of in 10:34, so here they desire the "better country." They seek a "homeland" or place that is their native environment, yet it remains ahead and is identified as a "heavenly one."

Eventually Jesus will be identified as the "author and perfecter of faith" (12:2). Like the "great cloud of witnesses" (12:1), he has struggled and suffered. This suffering servant "endured the cross, despising its shame," and did so "for the joy set before him" (12:2). Likely alluding to the promise of Isaiah 53:10, the author here portrays the struggle of faith as fixed upon a heavenly hope on the far side of suffering. Shaped by the prophetic imagination of Isaiah, wherein the servant suffers before finding his joy fulfilled, the author commends Jesus himself as sojourning obediently and selflessly precisely because he is heavenly minded. It is not surprising that Hebrews reads Jesus and the Old Testament saints in this way, for this is a remarkably regular dynamic plain to readers of the Old Testament, namely, that heavenly hope sustains the people of Israel through seasons of difficulty.[19]

Not surprisingly, Christians in various situations of oppression and struggle have cherished the heavenly minded intonations of the biblical testimony. African American spirituals serve as emblems of this kind of Israel-like spirituality wherein spiritual fortitude is instilled by vivid claims to living

19. Walter Brueggemann draws out the significance of both "energizing memories" and "radical hopes" for the ongoing practice of prophecy in ancient Israel in *The Prophetic Imagination*, 2nd ed. (Minneapolis: Fortress, 2001), see especially 59–80.

hope.[20] Celestial concern was not a privilege possessed only by the master class but marked the warp and woof of the spiritual undercurrents sustaining a people terrorized on earth. And this heavenly-mindedness continued to mark the piety and preaching of leaders like Martin Luther King Jr. in their leadership of the civil rights movements of the 1960s.[21] Spiritual resolve was not ornamental or instrumental but constitutive to the kind of witness maintained by King and other Christian activists.[22] Justice ultimately demands love as a motivating impulse, thus affection for the "better country" (Heb 11:16) must be instilled and formed, drawn out and sustained. Far from distracting from concern for justice and mercy in the earthly city, then, heavenly-mindedness may well provide the oxygen and energy by which it proceeds.

Indeed, we must remember that heavenly-mindedness does not excuse one from other actions, though it does re-order one's

20. See especially Howard Thurman, *Deep River: Reflections on the Religious Insight of Certain of the Negro Spirituals* (New York: Harper, 1955).

21. See especially Martin Luther King Jr., "A Time to Break Silence," in *I Have a Dream: Writings and Speeches That Changed the World*, ed. James M. Washington (San Francisco: HarperSanFrancisco, 1992), 139–40.

22. More recently, this kind of spiritual call to conversion and recalibration of hope and desire is read by even the sympathetic as either ornamental or instrumental. So, for example, E. J. Dionne paraphrases this call as a concern for conversion in the simple sense of believing one can win over one's critics in a conversation with David Brooks and Krista Tippett (see http://www.onbeing.org/program/david-brooks-and-ej-dionne-sinfulness-hopefulness-and-the-possibility-of-politics/transcript): "And there was a spirit in that form of Christianity that was, on the one hand, militant and demanding of justice. But on the other hand, the preaching of Martin Luther King was very much about conversion and redemption. And King actually believed you could convert adversaries. And we have very little of a sense that conversion is possible now in our political conversation. And conversion is a two-way street. People have to change themselves as they engage with each other." While Dionne's concern for civic conversation and the good of the earthly city is worthwhile, it nonetheless pales next to the need to address spiritual death and its connection to the heavenly city (as was done regularly by Martin Luther King Jr.).

loves and, thus, one's witness. Heavenly-mindedness provokes a deeper sense of lament and anger at that which frustrates us, naming it not only as pernicious market forces, psychological disorder, breakdown in family systems, or political disquiet, but as that truly pugnacious reality that can only be called sin or spiritual violence.[23] Heavenly-mindedness, then, turns up the volume on our moral register so that we are more alert to the pains of our precious sisters and brothers. Heavenly-mindedness not only cues us up to observe and feel such juxtapositions between the blueprints of God's kingdom and the experience of each day but also motivates us toward acts of self-sacrifice for the sake of the common good. By fixing our affections and hopes upon something deeper and more lasting, it frees us to give up what is ours for the sake of others.

The Structure of the Book: On Catholic Retrieval and Evangelical Reform in Dogmatic Theology

Eschatology in the twentieth and twenty-first centuries, especially in the Reformed theological tradition, has sought to attest to the earthy character of our hope and to draw out its ethical consequences in a fresh and vital way. To the extent that this has led back to biblical testimonies and forward to an authentic Christian imagination about self and world before God, this is all well and good. But, oftentimes, this eschatological frame has been too narrow (what Charles Taylor has termed an "immanent frame") and has thereby cropped God out of the picture, at least ultimately speaking. God has been instrumentalized and ends have been immanentized.

---

23. It is telling here that Cornel West has repeatedly identified "spiritual blackout" as the great struggle of the modern West, moving beyond thinly material, political, ideological, or psychological categories to something deeper and resolutely theological (which then serves as a fount of ills in those other registers).

My argument proceeds by way of two analytic moves: from hope to life, and from retrieval toward reform. It will benefit readers to sketch a bit of what is meant by each movement before proceeding further. First, we seek to retrieve classical Christian eschatology and ethics. Hope and life have been entangled in the Christian tradition, and so we divide the book into two parts—hope (eschatology) and life (ascetical ethics)—as a heuristic device and not a strict dichotomy. We will first consider ways in which we need to attend more carefully to a theological and even theocentric eschatology. We will then trace out ethical implications this living hope has for ascetical theology in various facets, most notably heavenly-mindedness and self-denial. Both parts are interjections in the ongoing conversation of Christian eschatology and ethics, seeking to reorient a conversation that has veered off the classical path for about a century now. The book does not seek to address, much less argue for, every component of a Christian doctrine of last things or a moral theology. This book is a theological infusion of crucial nutrients, not a holistic or regular diet.

Retrieval and renewal will shape the way we proceed in each area, suggesting that we listen best to Scripture when engaging with the church to which it was addressed and in which we receive it. Each part of the book, then, begins with retrieval.[24] In the first part we will describe the need to return a theocentric focus upon the beatific vision of God to our eschatology, over against the dominance of earthy aspects in recent neo-Calvinist theology. In the second part we will seek to portray the systemic significance of ascetical theology and heavenly-mindedness for

24. For exposition of a theology of retrieval, see especially Michael Allen and Scott R. Swain, *Reformed Catholicity: The Promise of Retrieval for Theology and Biblical Interpretation* (Grand Rapids: Baker Academic, 2015); see also John Webster, "Ressourcement Theology and Protestantism," in *Ressourcement: A Movement for Renewal in Twentieth-Century Catholic Theology*, ed. Gabriel Flynn and Paul D. Murray (Oxford: Oxford University Press, 2011), 482–94, and Darren Sarisky, ed., *Theologies of Retrieval: An Exploration and Appraisal* (London: T & T Clark, 2017).

classical Christian theology (drawing especially on patristic and Puritan writers), attempting to demonstrate its entanglements with facets of Christian faith and practice across the board. The catholic tradition is not homogenous in either area, though we do note some core concerns shared across the board (often over against modern tendencies) as well as some pivotal lines played by figures located within that classical orchestra.

The book is not only an argument for retrieval, however, and so it moves on toward assessing and extending reforms within that catholic tradition. So, second, we draw out the ways in which the Reformed theological tradition has reformed those basic Christian tenets. We will suggest that our theocentric eschatology must be centered on the vision of God (*visio Dei*) but that Reformed Trinitarian theology (along the lines suggested by John Owen) characterizes the visibility of God in a specifically Christological key. In the second part we will trace the ways in which John Calvin affirmed and framed ascetical theology, by attesting to self-denial as the central principle of the Christian life but also by insisting that it be normed by Holy Scripture and understood in light of our prior justification in Christ. In seeking to honor the specificity of Christ as the ultimate manifestation of God and the doubled grace of the gospel, we will argue for a refinement of the catholic doctrine of the beatific vision and the Christian practice of ascetic self-denial that better comports with these reformational principles of *solus Christus* and *sola fide*.

We begin then by considering the Christian hope before turning to address the way it prompts a particular way of life for those who entrust themselves to its promise.

In the End, God

Retrieving a Theological Eschatology

Eschatology came of age in the twentieth century in many ways. In that century Karl Barth said that any theology that is not wholly eschatological has nothing at all to do with Jesus Christ. In that century Ernst Käsemann argued that apocalyptic is the mother of all theology. Such claims for the importance of eschatology have been matched by new emphases regarding the substance of eschatology. And, perhaps more than any other person, Jürgen Moltmann has insisted that eschatology suffuses the Christian faith, and invigorates the moral and political imagination, with hope. Within the sphere of influence of Dutch Reformed theology as well—especially that based on the work of Abraham Kuyper and the so-called neo-Calvinism of the late nineteenth and early twentieth centuries—eschatology has been a major area of study. Proposed reforms in eschatology get at the nature of Christian hope and its *telos* (eternal life in heaven? new heavens and new earth?). Watchwords of this new emphasis can be identified: "embodied," "earthy," "cosmic," and "holistic."

Reform can be productive or parasitic. Theologically speaking, attempts to revitalize a doctrine, practice, or church sometimes lead to flourishing by way of deepening. But reforms can also be so intently or myopically focused as to lead to the unintended loss of a wider theological context and of confessional integrity. The danger of polemics in theological debate, then, is not only a matter of tone (whether loving or vindictive) and of content (whether true or false) but also of breadth (whether well balanced or narrow). Too many times, potentially prophetic words misfire because they are separated from a wider doctrinal commitment to the whole counsel of God. In such cases, a reform (perhaps a needful and good reform) takes a parasitic turn and eats away at the substance of the doctrine, confession, practice, or church. Should modern reforms to Christian eschatological hope be viewed as productive or as parasitic? How can we steer them toward the former and away from the latter?

Hope grasps at the future, but a serious Christian hope for our times also needs to reach back to the past.[1] The present chapter argues that contemporary Reformed theology, or at least the segment thereof that is heavily influenced by the neo-Calvinists or by the Kuyperian tradition, tends at times to maintain and extend its Reformed distinctiveness at the cost of its catholic substance. This forgetfulness is symptomatic not only of historical amnesia but of biblical dislocation. In several prominent recent accounts, central elements of the Kuyperian vision have been articulated in such a way that the center of our faith—the God who is with us (Immanuel)—goes missing at the finale. To regain a genuine Reformed catholicity, we need to retrieve an eschatology that is unabashedly and substantively theological.

Not that the neo-Calvinist emphasis upon the universality of Christ's lordship is wrong; far from it, for it too is exegetically vital and theologically central. Nor that the Augustinianism of the Kuyperians, with its testimony to Christ's reign throughout history and his providential governance of all things unto their blessed end, is misguided; again, nothing could be more

---

1. See Michael Allen and Scott Swain, *Reformed Catholicity: The Promise of Retrieval for Theology and Biblical Interpretation* (Grand Rapids: Baker Academic, 2015); cf. the various proposals in Darren Sarisky, ed., *Theologies of Retrieval: An Exploration and Appraisal* (London: T & T Clark, 2017).

appropriate and fundamental in reading the witness of both the prophets and the apostles. But the neo-Calvinist emphasis often forecloses other lines of scriptural teaching that have marked the church's life and ministry through the centuries. Kuyperians have been unduly suspicious of these teachings as well. In particular, Kuyperian eschatology has so emphasized the earthiness of our Christian hope that it has sometimes lost sight of broader biblical priorities and has consequently undercut the catholic tradition's emphasis upon communion with God and the ultimate bliss of the beatific vision. While Kuyperians have maintained an Augustinian emphasis upon God's grace and Christ's lordship, which bring us to our designated end in the kingdom of God, they have sometimes let slip the precise content of that end, namely, the presence of the triune God. We need to be wary, therefore, of unwittingly falling into an eschatological naturalism that speaks of God instrumentally (as a means to, or instigator of, an end) but fails to confess communion with God as our one true end (in whom alone any other things are to be enjoyed).

Lord of All:
The Kuyperian Reform of Christian Cosmology

Neo-Calvinism has shaped the Reformed theological world like no other movement in the late nineteenth and twentieth centuries. Largely owing to the instigation of Abraham Kuyper and to the analysis of Herman Bavinck, the Dutch Reformed theological vision has had inestimable impact far beyond the borders of the Netherlands or even of its immigrant churches elsewhere. Reformed theologians in other geographic, cultural, and denominational backgrounds have been resourced by Dutch Reformed theologians, ranging from Kuyper to Bavinck to Berkouwer to Hoekema.[2] In re-

2. For reference only to the remarkable impact of this tradition upon

cent years N. T. Wright has advanced Kuyperian principles in his many academic and popular writings, extending the influence of the tradition much more widely in his prolific work.[3]

Further, the tradition has had a catholic ripple effect in various ways. No doubt, the most intellectually respected movement from the Reformed world of late has been that of "Reformed epistemology" as developed by Alvin Plantinga.[4] Nicholas Wolterstorff has established himself as one of the most significant philosophers of recent decades, participating in conversations on a range of topics including the doctrine of God, aesthetics, justice, and the doctrine of divine revelation.[5] Both Plantinga and Wolterstorff have been Gifford lecturers, perhaps the highest mark of academic distinction in their field.

Not only in the highest echelons of philosophical inquiry but also in the grassroots movements of Christian education, the Dutch Reformed neo-Calvinist vision has spread like wildfire. Many primary and secondary schools now operate with an awareness of God's sovereignty or lordship over all things, of the calling to take captive every thought to Christ, and of the

Reformed theology in the United States of America, see James D. Bratt, *Dutch Calvinism in Modern America: A History of a Conservative Subculture* (Grand Rapids: Eerdmans, 1984), and the essays in part 2 of David F. Wells, *Reformed Theology in America: A History of Its Modern Development* (Grand Rapids: Baker, 1997), 115–86.

3. Wright himself has noted the influence of persons related to the neo-Calvinist Institute of Christian Studies in Toronto during his formative years in Canada in the 1980s.

4. Alvin Plantinga, *Warrant: The Current Debate* (New York: Oxford University Press, 1993); Alvin Plantinga, *Warrant and Proper Function* (New York: Oxford University Press, 1993); Alvin Plantinga, *Warranted Christian Belief* (New York: Oxford University Press, 2000).

5. See, e.g., Nicholas Wolterstorff, *Reason within the Bounds of Religion*, 2nd ed. (Grand Rapids: Eerdmans, 1988); Nicholas Wolterstorff, *Art in Action: Toward a Christian Aesthetic* (Grand Rapids: Eerdmans, 1987); Nicholas Wolterstorff, *Justice: Rights and Wrongs* (Princeton: Princeton University Press, 2010); and Nicholas Wolterstorff, *Divine Discourse: Philosophical Reflections on the Claim That God Speaks* (Cambridge: Cambridge University Press, 1995).

need, therefore, to think systemically about Christian formation and education. Recent criticisms by James K. A. Smith of
neo-Calvinist worldview education only illustrate the strength
of the movement inasmuch as they offer qualifications and contexts for its furtherance (not its demolition, as some misinformed
readers of Smith surmise).[6] And institutions with no specifically
Reformed commitments (e.g., Wheaton College) are marked by
philosophies of education that owe much to the emphases of the
neo-Calvinists, as evidenced by the programmatic statements issued previously by Arthur Holmes and more recently by Duane
Litfin.[7] Evangelicals at Wheaton and other schools have not all
gone Dutch, of course, but it takes little detective work to see the
lessons learned from the Kuyperians. I experienced the strengths
of this neo-Calvinist approach in my studies not only at Wheaton College (for multiple degrees) but also in a Christian school
founded by the Dutch Reformed in Miami, Florida, of all places.
When a movement from the Netherlands and the Dutch Midwest
has reached the "capital of Latin America," one can see something
of its wide cultural influence.

What have the neo-Calvinists given to this wider world of
academe and its various pockets or institutions of culture making? It is not inaccurate to suggest that the Kuyperian advance

6. See James K. A. Smith, *Desiring the Kingdom: Worship, Worldview,
and Cultural Formation*, Cultural Liturgies 1 (Grand Rapids: Baker Academic,
2009); James K. A. Smith, *Imagining the Kingdom: How Worship Works*, Cultural Liturgies 2 (Grand Rapids: Baker Academic, 2013); and especially the
following responses to reviews of *Desiring the Kingdom*: James K. A. Smith,
"Worldview, Sphere Sovereignty, and *Desiring the Kingdom*: A Guide for (Per-
plexed) Reformed Folk," *Pro Rege* 39, no. 4 (June 2011): 15–24; James K. A.
Smith, "From Christian Scholarship to Christian Education [Response to a
Review Symposium on *Desiring the Kingdom*]," *Christian Scholar's Review* 39
(2010): 229–32; and James K. A. Smith, "Two Cheers for Worldview: A Response to Thiessen," *Journal of Education and Christian Belief* 14 (2010): 55–58.

7. Arthur Holmes, *The Idea of a Christian College*, rev. ed. (Grand Rapids: Eerdmans, 1987); Duane Litfin, *Conceiving the Christian College* (Grand
Rapids: Eerdmans, 2004).

was a distinctly Reformed extension of certain reformational truths heralded by Martin Luther and John Calvin regarding the doctrines of creation, of humanity, and of vocation. Kuyperians have responded to the later temptation of modernity and its relocation of the religious in the private sphere by reaffirming and elaborating upon those reformers' teaching on the glory of the ordinary. In the hands of the Kuyperians, the sacred/secular dichotomy has been critiqued, reminding countless modern Christians that all of life is to be lived as unto the Lord (1 Cor 10:31).

Further, we must note that the Kuyperians have rooted these expositions of created reality in a deeper matter: the doctrine of the triune God. Perhaps no one is as impressive in this regard as that great dogmatician, Herman Bavinck. In his 1904 essay "The Future of Calvinism," he attempted to express the core commitments of the movement:

> The root principle of this Calvinism is the confession of God's absolute sovereignty. Not one special attribute of God, for instance His love or justice, His holiness or equity, but God Himself as such in the unity of all His attributes and perfection of His entire Being is the point of departure for the thinking and acting of the Calvinist. From this root principle everything that is specifically Reformed may be derived and explained. It was this that led to the sharp distinction between what is God's and creature's, to belief in the sole authority of the Holy Scriptures, in the all-sufficiency of Christ and His word, in the omnipotence of the work of grace. Hence also the sharp distinction between the divine and human in the Person and the two natures of Christ, between the external internal call, between the sign and the matter signified in the sacrament. From this source likewise sprang the doctrine of the absolute dependence of the creature,

as it is expressed in the Calvinistic confessions in regard to providence, foreordination, election, the inability of man. By this principle also the Calvinist was led to the use of that through-going consistent theological method, which distinguishes him from Romanist and other Protestant theologians. Not only in the whole range of his theology, but also outside of this, in every sphere of life and science, his effort aims at the recognition and maintenance of God as God over against all creatures. In the work of creation and regeneration, in sin and grace, in Adam and Christ, in the Church and the sacraments, it is in each case God who reveals and upholds His sovereignty and leads it to triumph notwithstanding all disregard and resistance. There is something heroic and grand and imposing in this Calvinistic conception. Viewed in its light the whole course of history becomes a gigantic contest, in which God carries through His sovereignty, and makes it, like a mountain stream, overcome all resistance in the end, bringing the creature to a willing or unwilling, but in either case unqualified, recognition of His divine glory. From God all things are, and accordingly they all return to Him. He is God and remains God now and forever; Jehovah, the Being, the one that was and is and that is to come.

For this reason the Calvinist in all things recurs upon God, and does not rest satisfied before he has traced back everything to the sovereign good-pleasure of God as its ultimate and deepest cause. He never loses himself in the appearance of things, but penetrates to their realities. Behind the phenomena he searches for the noumena, the things that are not seen, from which the things visible have been born. He does not take his stand in the midst of history, but out of time ascends into the heights of eternity. History is naught but the gradual unfolding of what to God is an eternal present. For his heart, his thinking, his life, the Calvinist cannot find rest in these terrestrial things, the sphere of what is becoming, changing, forever passing by. From the process of salvation he therefore recurs upon the decree of salvation, from history to the idea. He does not remain in the outer court of the temple, but seeks to enter into the innermost sanctuary.[8]

The elaboration extends quite far, of course, but it centers always upon God. While Kuyperianism may be most noteworthy in the integrity of created reality, which it honors and upholds over against the recurring temptations of gnostic or escapist metaphysics, eschatology, and ethics, Bavinck argues that the unique feature of this (and the wider Calvinist) tradition is the doctrine of God applied consistently. He has not argued that the doctrine of God itself is distinctive; rather, its consistent connection to and rule over all other areas of inquiry distinguishes this approach to faith and practice from all comers. For the Calvinist all things recur to God; the neo-Calvinist insists that the *novum* of the kingdom is precisely this universal and ultimate recurrence: Christ is making all things new (Rev 21:5). To think well, then, of the kingdom or of our civic responsibilities in Christ's various domains, we must always trace matters back from the realm of economics or gender or politics or knowing to God himself.

One example of this connection between the Trinitarian material of the faith and its methodological application across the dogmatic *loci* occurs in the realm of eschatology. Inasmuch as God created humanity to be the image of God (Gen 1:26–27) and has restored humanity to that same image in Christ Jesus (Rom 8:29), the neo-Calvinists have insisted that we must see the con-

8. Herman Bavinck, "The Future of Calvinism," *Presbyterian and Reformed Review* 5, no. 17 (1894). It can be found online at http://scdc.library .ptsem.edu/mets/mets.aspx?src=BR1894517&div=1.

nection between creation and eschatology.[9] They have expanded upon this further by noting ways in which the biblical writings express our hope in Christ in forms that are creaturely, embodied, and earthy. Whether through returning to prophetic texts like Isaiah 60 and their teaching regarding the future destiny of the ships of Tarshish, or by means of honoring the canonical closure found only in the depiction of the New Jerusalem in Revelation 21–22, the Kuyperians have led the way in articulating a this-worldly hope for Christians.[10]

The Earthy Hope:
The Kuyperian Reform of Christian Eschatology

The Kuyperian advance has focused at great length upon eschatology and the ways in which it connects to other topics: creation, humanity, image of God, and ethics among them. Perhaps no book so extensively illustrates this commitment as J. Richard Middleton's much-heralded *A New Heaven and a New Earth: Reclaiming Biblical Eschatology*.[11] It will repay our efforts to note his exposition, his forms of argument, and his application to Christian faith and practice. Only after paying due attention to his own argument might it be helpful to present a statement of caution.

9. For a masterful account of how created nature and eschatological *telos* must be brought together, see Brian G. Mattson, *Restored to Our Destiny: Eschatology and the Image of God in Herman Bavinck's Reformed Dogmatics*, Studies in Reformed Theology 21 (Leiden: Brill, 2012); see also John Webster, "Eschatology and Anthropology," in *Word and Church: Essays in Christian Dogmatics* (Edinburgh: T & T Clark, 2001), 263–86.

10. See, e.g., Richard Mouw, *When the Kings Come Marching In: Isaiah and the New Jerusalem*, rev. ed. (Grand Rapids: Eerdmans, 2002), esp. 13–42.

11. J. Richard Middleton, *A New Heaven and a New Earth: Reclaiming Biblical Eschatology* (Grand Rapids: Baker Academic, 2014). Future references to this work are noted in the text by page numbers in parentheses.

Middleton's book itself addresses a polemical target, what he calls the "problem of otherworldly hope." As he surveys the heightened eschatological inquiry of the modern era, he avers: "The twentieth century has seen more intense focus on eschatology than ever before. Yet much of this eschatological reflection has been confused and inchoate, conflating an unbiblical impetus to transcend earthly life with the biblical affirmation of earthly life. This is true among both professional theologians and church members, and also among Christians of differing theological traditions" (15). He further focuses his target: "Although there are many New Testament texts that Christians often read as if they teach a heavenly destiny, the texts do not actually say this" (14). Middleton consistently functions with a dichotomy: the spiritualist approach of otherworldly hope says heaven is our destiny, while the biblical witness says heaven is not our final homeland.

Repeatedly Middleton notes a seeming tension laden in the heart of the church's lived theology and explicitly in the testimony of some of her most significant theologians. "While the traditional doctrine of the resurrection of the body is usually affirmed, this typically stands in some tension with the idea of an atemporal, immaterial realm" (23; see also 12). The movement of his text attempts to alleviate this tension by presenting what he repeatedly terms a "holistic eschatology." The argument moves in five parts: from creation to eschaton; holistic salvation in the Old Testament; the New Testament's vision of cosmic renewal; problem texts for holistic eschatology; and the ethics of the kingdom.

Middleton's rebuttal takes the form of sketching "the coherent biblical theology (beginning in the Old Testament) that culminates in the New Testament's explicit eschatological vision of the redemption of creation" (15). Indeed, "this holistic vision of God's intent to renew or redeem creation is perhaps the Bible's best-kept secret" (24). Middleton surveys the hymnody of the church to note how heaven has become the destiny of Christians, at least as expressed in their songs (in a section entitled "Singing Lies in

Church"; 27–30). Then he turns to offer a brief description of how this "idea of a heavenly destiny" had its origins in the early Christian church's absorption of middle Platonism through the work of Plotinus, especially in the way that he "explicitly identified the ascent to the divine with the turn inward, thereby initiating a Western form of mysticism that has reverberated throughout the church in the Middle Ages and even into the modern period" (33).

It is worth noting that Middleton cites not a single text from the patristic period to demonstrate this capitulation to or absorption of middle Platonism. The only reference to anything Christian is a footnote stating that Augustine (in his *Confessions*) mentions that Plotinus was viewed as being a genuine Platonist. At the same time, Middleton does note the similarity of the spiritual vision of middle Platonism with the earlier Old Testament teaching on *sheol*, which would seem to raise the question about why this spiritual vision need necessarily be alien to the canonical witness or the theology of the people of God given that it is present within the bounds of the Old Testament. The argument here seems to suffer, then, from too little documentation and too much opposition (33n33; 31).

The biblical theology presented by Middleton moves from Genesis to Apocalypse, attempting to show a consistent portrait of God's lordly design for human flourishing in this creaturely habitat and according to our vocation as *imago Dei*.[12] Middleton first sketches the human calling as God's image, and then he outlines the biblical plotline through which that calling finds its subjects identified, problematized, given new hope, restored, and, eventually in glory, fully renewed. A hermeneutical principle is enunciated along the way: "We are prone to miss the amazing scope of God's redemption, and especially its full-bodied, this-

12. A topic on which Middleton has written at length elsewhere: J. Richard Middleton, *The Liberating Image: The* Imago Dei *in Genesis* 1 (Grand Rapids: Brazos, 2005).

worldly character, if we do not read the New Testament with the worldview of the Old Testament as our basis and guide" (78). The maxim: read the New in terms of the Old.

This hermeneutical approach bears fruit in the way that Middleton treats the exodus as "paradigm of salvation" (ch. 4). He offers a judgment regarding the meaning and significance of that emblematic event in ancient history: "The most fundamental meaning of salvation in Scripture is twofold: it is God's *deliverance* of those in a situation of need from that which impedes their well-being, resulting in their *restoration* to wholeness" (79, emphasis original). He expands on how the exodus illustrates the holistic character of God's beneficent acts: "The first thing we should notice about the exodus is that it constitutes the sociopolitical deliverance of a historical community from a real, concrete situation of oppression. The exodus resists any 'spiritualizing' of salvation, keeping it firmly rooted in life in this world" (80). Indeed, "this paradigmatic work of YHWH on behalf of Israel establishes a movement toward this-worldly flourishing as the goal of salvation," which can then be traced through the cycles of teaching found in the Law, Wisdom, and Prophets (95). He notes that Deuteronomic teaching on covenantal blessings and curses shows how (dis)obedience before God has earthly consequences for good or ill; indeed, he says that "Babylonian exile is the ultimate consequence for unfaithfulness to YHWH" (97).

Middleton notes that prophetic language in the Old Testament takes hyperbolic form to demonstrate "forcefully and vividly . . . that God is the agent behind these events and that radical judgment is necessary to accomplish salvation" (121). In a later chapter focused on seemingly problematic texts for his thesis regarding holistic eschatology (e.g., Heb 12:26–28; 2 Pet 3:10–12), he repeatedly makes the same point: apostolic testimony that seems to suggest the destruction or annihilation of the present world and its replacement with another serves hyperbolically to signal the need for God's apocalyptic intervention in restoring this present world.[13]

When he turns to the New Testament witnesses, Middleton suggests that there is a continuity of belief but a novel emphasis upon life after death. Indeed, "one of the contrasts between the Old Testament and the New Testament is their understanding of the afterlife. In contrast to the centrality of the resurrection in the New Testament (and late Second Temple Judaism), the Old Testament does not typically place any significant hope in life after death."[14] Middleton argues that Christ is our forerunner as he now rules earth from heaven and will one day return to earth to rule finally and fully. He then surveys a number of texts that portray the object of Christ's restorative work to be "all things" on earth that shall become like unto heaven.[15] He concludes by asking: "But what are redeemed people to do in the new creation? Just as we have to get rid of the unbiblical idea of 'going to heaven' as our final destiny, so we need to drop pious ideas of a perpetual worship service as our ultimate purpose in the eschaton" (174).

13. Middleton, *A New Heaven and a New Earth*, ch. 9. However, Middleton does not employ this exegetical observation alone against the charge that these texts contradict his emphasis on holistic eschatology and the restoration of all things in Christ. He also makes a number of contextual points with regard to the diverse texts.

14. Middleton, *A New Heaven and a New Earth*, 132–33. Perplexingly, Middleton here cites a volume co-authored by Kevin Madigan and Jon Levenson, *Resurrection: The Power of God for Christians and Jews* (New Haven: Yale University Press, 2008). One of the most notable facets of this text is its insistence that the Old Testament (or Hebrew Bible, as Levenson calls it) testifies to resurrection far more than is typically acknowledged; so also Levenson's larger volume, *Resurrection and the Restoration of Israel: The Ultimate Victory of the God of Life* (New Haven: Yale University Press, 2006). This Jewish scholar commends a hermeneutical approach to the Old Testament scriptures that follows the model of Jesus (e.g., in Luke 24:46) more closely than does the neo-Calvinist!

15. Middleton, *A New Heaven and a New Earth*, chs. 7 and 8, respectively.

Retrieving Classical Christian Eschatology

God is not only instigator of but also integral to our hope. That, we may say, is the watchword of classical Christian hope in its myriad forms through the centuries. We do well to unpack the statement and its moorings in exegetical reasoning, though, so that we can appreciate its relationship to these more recent neo-Calvinist iterations of Christian eschatology.[16]

Before we consider the end, we do well to pay attention to the beginning. The first creation account (Gen 1:1–2:4) tells of many grand and glorious things: the division of the land and the seas, of day and night, and the many inventions of species and selves. It culminates not with production, however, but with presence: God dwells in the midst of his people, resting there on that seventh day. Recent commentators have helped us note the temple imagery present there, showing that God is fashioning a world fit for his dwelling, much as a temple will later be made as his home. And this is neither merely another feature of the creation account nor the form of its telling; no, God's special presence with his people is the finale of the entire creation story.[17]

---

16. For a sketch of the doctrine through the centuries, see K. E. Kirk, *The Vision of God: The Christian Doctrine of the* Summum Bonum (London: Longmans, Green, & Co., 1931). Kirk's account rightly ties eschatology to ethics, though it does not always demonstrate the plasticity needed to appreciate the varying ways in which that link can be construed over the centuries. For all the benefits of Kirk's panoramic sketch, a fresh account of the historical development is much needed (and Hans Boersma's *Seeing God: The Beatific Vision in Christian Tradition* [Grand Rapids: Eerdmans, 2018] moves further in this direction).

17. See Jon D. Levenson, "The Temple and the World," *Journal of Religion* 64, no. 3 (1984): 275–98; Gordon Wenham, "Sanctuary Symbolism in the Garden of Eden Story," in *Proceedings of the Ninth World Congress of Jewish Studies* (Jerusalem: World Union of Jewish Studies, 1986), 19–25; Gregory K. Beale, *The Temple and the Church's Mission: A Biblical Theology of the Dwelling Place of God*, New Studies in Biblical Theology 15 (Downers Grove, IL: IVP Academic, 2004).

The end of the Christian Bible is not all that different. The terminology has shifted somewhat, with language of a city and of buildings inserted among the portraits of gardens and rivers. The separation of the righteous (in Christ) and the wicked (apart from Christ) marks this grand and glorious portrait; the glitz and glimmer involve not only the natural order and architectural beauty of the New Jerusalem but also the relational harmony of a land without tears. And yet, again, the central word is not one of newness but of nearness. The great promise is, "Behold, the dwelling place of God is with man. He will dwell with them, and they will be his people, and God himself will be with them as their God" (Rev 21:3). The centrality of this tenet may be seen not only in the way in which the one element missing in the picture is a temple, a place that would denote limits or restrictions upon the extent of God's dwelling or habitation (21:22–27), but also and especially in the final repetition of the good word: "Behold, I am coming soon" (22:12, 20).

These moments, which serve as bookends to redemptive history, not only tell us something about ourselves but ultimately reveal something fundamental about God, namely, that God is the Alpha and the Omega, that the triune one is the Beginning and the End. And, in thinking about Christian eschatology, we do well to keep in mind a fundamental rule of all Christian teaching, namely, that our emphases and priorities ought to be given and governed by God himself through his appointed instruments— the scriptural testimony of his prophets and apostles. Theology seeks not only right answers but also better questions.

Why might this rule be significant? Well, John Calvin suggested that each of us has a heart that is an idol-making factory.[18] In suggesting this, he was not simply talking like a lawyer (though

---

18. John Calvin, *Institutes of the Christian Religion*, ed. John T. McNeill, trans. Ford Lewis Battles, Library of Christian Classics 20 (Louisville: Westminster John Knox, 2006), 1:108 (I.xi.8).

he had been one), nor expressing a morose personality (though you might be morose if you had to flee through an open window from a violent mob in Paris). He was reflecting upon the biblical teaching that idolatry marks all people, not just the pagans of Egypt or of Canaan but even the liberated slaves at the foot of Mt. Sinai. Owing to zeal without knowledge, and left to ourselves, each of us is quite capable of worshiping the right God with the wrong golden calf.

Because we are sinners who continue to struggle with indwelling sin and live among a people of unclean lips, we require recalibration. The apostle Paul addresses this need famously in his words to the Romans: "Do not be conformed to this world, but be transformed by the renewal of your mind, that by testing you may discern what is the will of God, what is good and acceptable and perfect" (12:2). Knowing God's will does not come easily or naturally to those living east of Eden, even those saved by Christ. We first must present a stiff-arm to the culture, but we also must seek the renewal of our own minds as they are because we are not unaffected by the stain of sin. The transforming renewal of our minds occurs now as it did then, by being taken to school by the apostles: the formation that comes from learning of the works of God and the ways of God, the faith and practice that mark the evangelical community.[19]

The danger of idolatry lurks especially in the realm of eschatology. When we speak of eschatology, we are speaking of fundamental hopes and ultimate desires. Matters of priority and significance come right to the surface because we are addressing what has lasting meaning, value, and integrity in God's economy. Numerous

19. Compare the approach to such renewal in Sarah Coakley, *God, Sexuality, and the Self: An Essay "On the Trinity"* (Cambridge: Cambridge University Press, 2014), 33–65, with John Webster, "The Holiness of Theology," in *Holiness* (Grand Rapids: Eerdmans, 2003), 8–30, and Michael Allen, "Dogmatics as Ascetics," in *The Task of Dogmatics*, ed. Oliver Crisp and Fred Sanders (Grand Rapids: Zondervan Academic, 2017), 189–209.

errors can be identified in this eschatological realm: some have suggested that some superior race will eventually triumph; some that the truly faithful will gain the financial wealth; others that all world religions will be brought info final harmony. Each of these errors flows from some cultural and personal ideal being given independent significance in a way not acknowledged or upheld by (and oftentimes quite contradictory to) the teaching of Holy Scripture.

How will restoring a properly scriptural and doctrinal approach reshape our eschatology? We will recognize that God is not only the cause but also the center of our Christian hope.

First, God is the cause of our hope. The New Testament makes plain that faith and sight are juxtaposed (e.g., Heb 11:1). This distinction marks not simply the temporal nature of our hope (yet to come) but the generative source of our hope (as not being immanent or intrinsic). The Lord brings about what he has promised: the gates of hell will not prevail against the onward movement of Christ's church (Matt 16:18), and the commission to Christ's disciples will be fulfilled owing to the authoritative presence of their Lord unto the very end (Matt 28:19–20; note "I am with you always, to the end of the age"). Theologians have varied in how they articulate language of causality, whether taking it up and fashioning it to suit divine agency amidst a creaturely realm or suggesting that it be replaced or translated into another idiom like that of divine gift and provision. In either approach, however, they attempt to point to the singular agency of God in grounding our hope and in bringing what can now only be grasped by faith unto such reality and presence that it can be seen.

Second, God is the center of our hope. We see this in Jesus's comments regarding the practice of his disciples: they do not fast while he is there, though a time will come when they do so (Matt 9:14–15). Notice that Jesus does not offer just any circumstance as the criterion for deciding when one mourns and when one rejoices. Rather, his personal presence tilts the mood one way or another. He focuses on this matter of personal presence (of the nearness of the bridegroom) not because health, worldly peace, the clean conscience, relational unity, and the like do not matter. Rather, he focuses upon personal presence because it is primary—the word "Immanuel" (God with us) connects his teaching with the Alpha and Omega of Holy Scripture.

Whereas idolatry may take the form of instrumentalizing God—treating him as the liberator from captivity and the sovereign who brought one to prosperity, and then turning to worship in an illicit form—theology that seeks to follow the emphases of the Scriptures will be alert to the reality that at the end of God's grace is, ultimately, God. His creation, sustenance, instruction, patience, deliverance, reconciliation, forgiveness, resurrection, and so many other intermediate and unnamed kindnesses—they are all unto God. The gospel logic runs: "From him, through him, and to him are all things" (Rom 11:36). While our vision or enjoyment of heaven is a creaturely enjoyment—thus experienced in time and space and as embodied and social beings—its object is that one who is no creature but the Lord God Almighty; at least that was the testimony of Thomas Aquinas.[20]

In the end, then, heaven comes to earth. We do not hope for an angelic existence (see not only Ps 8 but also Heb 2:6–9), and we do not ultimately long to be absent from the body (though this is an appropriate intermediate hope: Phil 1:21–24). But Jesus taught us to pray in this way, aspiring unto heavenliness (Matt 6:10), and called us to seek first the kingdom of God—the realm in which God resides and rules—not all the other good things that accompany God's blessed presence (Matt 6:33). In the end, as in the beginning, God will be there.

20. Thomas Aquinas, *Summa theologiae*, Ia-IIæ, Q. 3, Art. 1, *Respondeo*: "man's ultimate end is uncreated good, namely God, who alone can fill the will of man to the brim because of his infinite goodness. Yet . . . man's ultimate end is a creaturely reality in him, for what is it but his coming to God and his joy with God . . . so then, with respect to its object or cause happiness is uncreated reality, while with respect to its essence it is a creaturely reality."

On Eschatological Naturalism

The sweep of Middleton's survey reaches from beginning to end, explicitly taking in all things and subsuming them under the sovereignty of the risen king Jesus. There is much to be commended in this volume: the diligent commitment to receiving the Old Testament Scriptures as an abiding word for today; the perception that the eschatological is not merely a component part of the Christian gospel but is woven throughout the biblical witness; the keen sense that one's *telos* and hope shape one's ethics; and, of course, the consistent concern to alert us to the Kuyperian advance regarding what is termed "holistic eschatology." To these material matters, we could add a number of formal strengths as well: an unwillingness to move far from exegetical argument; a sense of responsibility to address what may appear to be the strongest arguments against the central thesis; an extensive awareness of recent biblical scholarship; and a tone throughout that is marked by the cadence of hope, surely a necessity for any exposition of the Christian doctrine of last things. The patience to allow God's instruction through life with Israel to prepare us for the gift of Immanuel is also worthy of note, contrary to neo-Marcionite trends of recent decades.

And yet, Middleton's volume serves as a barometer of sorts for what I believe we must term eschatological naturalism and thereby illustrates a number of material and formal problems. First, the material matters. By eschatological naturalism, I refer very specifically to a theological approach that speaks of God instrumentally as a means or instigator of an end but fails to confess substantively that God's identity as our one true end (in whom only any other things are to be enjoyed). In other words, I do not refer to a theology that is naturalistic across the board but one that is naturalistic only in a targeted manner regarding eschatological confessions (or the lack thereof). In the hands of eschatological naturalism, the secondary is elevated to the primary position in terms of Christian hope, and that which is in fact primary is relegated (at best) to the fringes, if not outright dismissed. It is as though one focuses upon the ever-widening circumference of the sun's rays while committing oneself never to note its own fiery beauty and occasionally even jeering those who do for propagating lies.

For centuries, as we have seen, Christians have hoped for life forevermore with God. The cry of the apostle Paul was for the personal return of our Lord: "Our Lord, come!" (1 Cor 16:22). This personal hope of union with God has taken the shape of Christian expectation of the beatific vision of God in Christ. It has played such a role in Christian theology, both Catholic and Protestant, that prolegomena have routinely felt compelled to distinguish our present knowledge of God as that of faith from that which shall be ours when we are those blessed with God's presence that can be seen. Theologians ranging from Thomas Aquinas to Franciscus Junius worked with such programmatic distinctions, noting that the apogee of spiritual bliss comes only with the kingdom and the personal presence of the Lord, the one true object of our theological knowledge. This vision not only centered the discussion of our end and hope but filtered into these others topics, framing issues like epistemology in a particular eschatological hue.

While eschatology has moved front and center in twentieth-century Protestant theology, the beatific vision appears to have exited stage right. Brunner gave it a paragraph; Jenson a sentence; Barth nary a word. The absence is glaring in the face of the substantial place held by the doctrine of the beatific vision in classical faith and practice, where the beatific vision played a role in prolegomena (as the ultimate form of human knowledge of God), in eschatology (as the central hope of the Christian), and in ethics (as the driving force or motivation for ascetic discipline). Attention has fixed upon the environment, the body, and social relations (all of which are facets of a biblical eschatology), but oftentimes such concern has come at a cost and not infrequently with a smirk. The marginalization of the beatific vision from modern Protestant theology proves a remarkable case study and, I suggest, marks a fundamental problem with the earthy eschatology of the contemporary church.

Eschatological naturalism marginalizes the presence of God and regularly maligns the spiritual hope of earlier Christians. Middleton exemplifies both patterns.[21] He offers only very scattered and marginal reference to the presence of God as an element (much less the key element) in the kingdom of God.[22] Further, he repeatedly argues that Christians need to be retrained away from their notions of heaven as a personal union with God. In so doing he is not unique or pathbreaking, even if his rhetoric is at times stronger than others. Perhaps a signal marker of this tendency comes with the place or tone given to remarks on Matthew 6:10, wherein our Lord guides his disciplines to pray that God's will be done "on earth as it is in heaven." Middleton offers no assessment of the way in which heaven is not merely a substitute for earth but comes to be a qualification or characterization of the new earth.[23] Surely something has gone wrong when our primary tone for speaking of heaven is to note that it's not our hope rather than identifying our hope as being heaven and noting its presence eventually here in the new earth and the New Jerusalem.

A catholic context for Middleton's Reformed distinctives can be found close within his tradition, providing a more fitting

21. Notice, then, that my characterization of eschatological naturalism as a tendency in Reformed eschatology is not built simply upon arguments from silence, but upon that widespread silence paired with a regular pattern of criticisms directed at classical Christian eschatology (oftentimes brutal ones, suggesting that the church has regularly lied to its congregants regarding heaven, on which see Middleton, *A New Heaven and a New Earth*, 27–30).

22. Middleton, *A New Heaven and a New Earth*, 89–90, 107, 166–68, 172.

23. The closest that he comes to making this point is in noting that Terence Fretheim makes the point (Middleton, *A New Heaven and a New Earth*, 72n27).

and promising model for the path forward. Anthony Hoekema offered a compelling vision of the new earth as the final destination of Christians, who would only spend the intermediate state in an immaterial existence. But in doing so, he offered a positive account of the term "heaven" by noting how God unites the heavens and the earth: "Since God will make the new earth his dwelling place, and since where God dwells there heaven is, we shall then continue to be in heaven while we are on the new earth. For heaven and earth will then no longer be separated, as they are now, but will be one (see Rev 21:1–3)."[24] Hoekema's energies are then turned to describing the significance of the earthly locale of this heavenly state, a needful task and a remarkable distinctive of the neo-Kuyperian heritage that he shares with Middleton. But the adversarial rhetoric, the dismissive shoulder to centuries of piety, and the reductive approach to biblical imagery and vocabulary are all absent. Instead, Hoekema offers a relatively catholic

24. Anthony Hoekema, *The Bible and the Future* (Grand Rapids: Eerdmans, 1979), 274 (see also 285, where he offers an exposition of Rev 21:1–4). In a more recent publication, while the earthly blessings of the eschaton are acknowledged, it is noted that "salvation has a spiritual depth, which is its nucleus" (J. van Genderen and W. H. Velema, *Concise Reformed Dogmatics*, trans. Gerrit Bilkes and Ed M. van der Maas [Phillipsburg, NJ: Presbyterian & Reformed, 2008], 821 [see also 836–38 on life in communion with Christ in the hereafter, and 879–82 on eternal life with God]). James K. A. Smith has also offered preliminary comments on how Reformed and Christian engagement of modern secularism needs to avoid falling into an "exclusive humanism" that either omits or minimizes our transcendent fulfillment in God (*How [Not] to Be Secular: Reading Charles Taylor* [Grand Rapids: Eerdmans, 2014], 35–40, 48–51, 113–14). Interestingly, for all his focus upon the earthy and political kingdom, Moltmann does not avoid addressing spiritual communion with God under any number of theological categories, ranging from "fulfillment of space in the presence of God" to "the fullness of God and the feast of eternal joy" (see *The Coming of God: Christian Eschatology*, trans. Margaret Kohl [Minneapolis: Fortress, 1996]). In his programmatic comments about the shape of his eschatology, Moltmann argues that one must begin with the personal and move (sequentially through the order of knowing and, inversely, up the order of being) from the personal to the world to the body to the kingdom (xvi).

account of our hope that underlines a Reformed emphasis upon the earthiness of heaven's final resting place.

Unfortunately, Hoekema's catholicity in this regard is rare in the modern Dutch Reformed world, at least when it comes to eschatology this side of Kuyper. The great polemical concern of the greatest dogmatician of the Kuyperian tradition, Herman Bavinck, is spiritualism, a danger he sees rampant in the classical tradition and looming in much recent pietism. He admits that "present in the New Testament there is undoubtedly some spiritualization of Old Testament prophecy," noting the ways in which the double appearance of Christ requires some of his kingdom's characteristics to be true for a while only spiritually and then, upon his return, physically as well. "But this does not confine this blessedness to heaven. This cannot be the case as is basically evident from the fact that the New Testament teaches the incarnation of the Word and the physical resurrection of Christ; it further expects his physical return at the end of time and immediately thereafter has in view the physical resurrection of all human beings, especially that of believers." His assessment: "All this spells the collapse of spiritualism." Bavinck views this as a uniquely Protestant emphasis upon the renewal of creation as such, monasticism having symbolized the Eastern and Roman focus upon a purely supernatural hope, which he terms "abstract" and "exclusively transcendent." In summary, Bavinck notes that "the Reformation, going back to Scripture, in principle overcame this supernaturalistic and ascetic view of life." Even Bavinck, typically among the most catholic of Reformed theologians, turns adversarial when it comes to eschatology: the spiritual, the ascetic, the supernaturalistic are all maligned.[25]

25. The single qualifying remark made by Bavinck in this discussion notes that it is "misguided . . . to make the material into the chief component of future blessedness" (*Reformed Dogmatics*, 4 vols. [Grand Rapids: Baker Academic, 2002–2006], 4:720). Amen. Sadly, Bavinck's presentation, order, and rhetoric consistently convey the opposite.

The concern of the Kuyperian tradition can and should be appreciated. Gnosticism and dualism are real threats. The gospel is good news for us, not for angels or disembodied beings but for us: men and women made after the image of the triune God and remade in the image of Jesus of Nazareth. The apocalyptic portrait of our hope portrays a home: the New Jerusalem in the new heavens and new earth. Theologians and exegetes regularly and rightly lambast any notion that Christian hope is otherworldly or non-earthly (likened regularly in the literature to the naïve expectations of someday only playing harps up in the clouds).[26] Thus, no one wishes to shift to an eschatology that is ethereal or disembodied. I do not advocate a return to life prior to the remarkable witness of theologians like Bavinck. His biblical imagination, commitment to the full canonical scope of Scripture, and unswerving determination to let dogmatic eschatology shape Christian ethics are all to be commended and never to be forgotten. And yet it seems to me that one can (and many seem, unintentionally, to do so) herald something akin to Bavinck's Augustinian vision without capturing the very center of Augustine's eschatology (and that of the classical Christian consensus that marked at least the late patristic and medieval eras). Such an eschatological naturalism (unintentionally) focuses on the New Jerusalem rather than her chief occupant, forgetting that the best news of Christian bliss is not newness but nearness: "Behold, the dwelling place of God is with man" (Rev 21:3). Hence the repetition of the promise: "Behold, I am coming soon" (Rev 22:7, 12, 20). Middleton, along with significant others (most notably N. T. Wright), seems to have plunged into this trap, whether intentionally or unintentionally.[27]

26. It is worth noting, however, that Revelation 14:2 and 15:2 commend the vision of harp playing in eschatological bliss, so we do well to realize that while the end envisioned by Christian faith cannot be reduced to nothing but liturgy, it is certainly not less than liturgy. Worship is our end, albeit worship here on earth where heaven has made its eternal home.

27. See N. T. Wright, *Surprised by Hope: Rethinking Heaven, the Resur-*

Fortunately, a number of recent studies have suggested the need to retrieve riches from this ancient and medieval past regarding the special character of our Christian hope. For example, Matthew Levering and Hans Boersma have each presented an argument that recent eschatology and anthropology are too much focused on, or perhaps even restricted to, earthly concerns (e.g., a common target of theirs is the eschatological vision of N. T. Wright).[28] Levering seeks to retrieve the eschatological imagination of Thomas Aquinas, which he argues was shaped by the categories of Israel's Scriptures, rooted in the Greek and Latin patristic tradition, and expressed in his monastic vocation unto the poor and those in need of both daily bread and the bread of life. Boersma ranges much more widely, arguing for the need to return to a Christian-Platonist synthesis that is more otherworldly, drawing primarily upon patristic figures (most notably Gregory of Nyssa).[29]

---

rection, and the Mission of the Church (New York: HarperOne, 2008), though Wright does have the occasional positive comment about "heaven" meeting "earth" (e.g., 104–5). In a different vein, Christopher Morse emphasizes newness as apocalyptic inbreaking of the promised *futurum* of God, albeit bereft of a corresponding center in the personal presence of God or form shaped by the covenantal parameters for that fellowship as revealed in the scriptures of Israel, in so doing misperceiving or confusing the incommensurability of heaven's kingdom with its spontaneity (*The Difference Heaven Makes: Rehearsing the Gospel as News* [London: T & T Clark, 2010], esp. 108–11).

28. Matthew Levering, *Jesus and the Demise of Death: Resurrection, Afterlife, and the Fate of the Christian* (Waco, TX: Baylor University Press, 2012), 109–26; Hans Boersma, *Heavenly Participation: The Weaving of a Sacramental Tapestry* (Grand Rapids: Eerdmans, 2011). While I share their concerns regarding the reductively naturalistic eschatologies of Wright and others, I would have significant concerns about facets of their respective projects. For example, I disagree with some distinctively Roman aspects of Levering's approach, such as purgatory, and with Boersma's thoroughgoing proposal of a "sacramental ontology," which I think unintentionally undervalues the distinctive and particular place of the two sacraments given to the church by her Lord. Boersma certainly does not intend to undersell the distinction between cosmos and cult, but I think his phrasing fails to avoid doing so.

29. See also a more technical study: Hans Boersma, *Embodiment and*

Even more significant, perhaps, is the portrayal of Augustine's theology offered by Charles Mathewes in his sadly neglected but vital work, *A Theology of Public Life*.[30] In the course of offering a "dogmatics of public life," Mathewes draws from Augustine of Hippo a critique of our current anxiety about being otherworldly. Indeed, Mathewes shows that Augustine's great concern was not otherworldliness as such, but idolatry (which may be ethereal or material).[31] Thus, he rightly ties together a truly spiritual center to our hope with a demand for serious moral engagement now (noting that it will take the form of what Bavinck had only negative words for, a Protestant version of asceticism). The book proves so significant precisely because it offers a spiritually centered account of eschatology that, nonetheless, shows how being spiritually minded enables one to be of earthly (ethical and public) good. And it does so in the words and way of Augustine, the patron saint of so much twentieth-century Reformed eschatology.

Eschatological naturalism treats God as the sovereign instigator and cause of Christian hope, the almighty and gracious Lord who brings his kingdom to pass. But when it comes to describing or articulating that glory, it searches for other items, realities, and persons to mark its very nature: the shalom of the city, the redemption of creation, the resurrection of the body. Its ends can and have at times become naturalistic, limited to the horizontal or immanent frame (to use Charles Taylor's terminology). Of course, there is no logical reason that the confession of the resurrection of the body, or of social harmony, or of a renewed heavens and earth might prompt such theological forgetfulness when it comes to the end. And in its better forms (e.g., as in G. C. Berkouwer's *The Return of Christ*) the Kuyperian tradition has continued to affirm

---

Virtue in Gregory of Nyssa: An Anagogical Approach, Oxford Early Christian Studies (New York: Oxford University Press, 2013).

30. Charles Mathewes, *A Theology of Public Life*, Cambridge Studies in Christian Doctrine (Cambridge: Cambridge University Press, 2007).

31. Mathewes, *A Theology of Public Life*, 76–79.

the spiritual center of our hope amidst its broad reach into every nook and cranny of our cosmos, selves, and society.

The way forward in dogmatic eschatology should be Augustinian, and it should avoid both spiritualism and naturalism. Bavinck's reform to pietistic eschatology was needed and should be celebrated, but it must be held amidst a wider catholic matrix of eschatological hope than Bavinck himself articulates (or at least emphasizes). So our future thinking ought rather to follow the wisdom of Gregory and Augustine, of Thomas, and of later Protestants such as John Owen. These thinkers show that the special character of our hope as spiritual communion with God through Jesus Christ provides the means for honoring both heaven and earth. It must center upon God, but contain within it a vision of God renewing all things in him. Retrieving the doctrine of the beatific vision—and noting the spiritual communion to which it is meant to alert us—may be a powerful resource for better thinking of our Christian hope in a Christ-centered key. Here, as much as anywhere else, we benefit from a vision for theological retrieval and, thus, from a retrieval of the importance of that blessed vision that is yet to be ours.

On Polemics, Theological Systems, Metaphorical Language, and Reformed Movements

Eschatological naturalism presents a particular vision of God's kingdom, wherein the triune God sovereignly brings about that kingdom but then seemingly slides off stage-right upon its culmination. Thankfully, references to the presence of God continue to pop up among those marked by this tendency; even Middleton does at times refer to or speak of the eschatological presence of God.[32] But the movement as such and its rhetoric—found in ex-

32. Middleton, *A New Heaven and a New Earth*, 89–90, 107, 166–68, 172.

plicit claims and emphasized through repetition, shrill cadence, and organization—point in a very different direction: to a hope that does not center upon God and too often goes without mention of anything specifically Christian in its substance.[33] A number of observations might be made about the way in which eschatological naturalism relates to historical polemics, to hermeneutics of the canon, to theological method, and to ecclesiastical life in the Reformed world. In hopes that the neo-Calvinist reform might contribute productively rather than parasitically in the future, such related matters deserve further exploration by way of conclusion.

First, one of the motivations for eschatological naturalism is polemics, specifically a riposte to the dispensationalism and rapture theology fostered in the late nineteenth century and beyond. Indeed, the appendix offered by Middleton regarding "whatever happened to the new earth?" surveys church history, addressing Origen, Augustine, Thomas, and the reformers, but it locates only black hats with any specific textual reference when it arrives at the rise of modern dispensationalism. One wonders if the polemic has not been expanded beyond reason, as if the whole classical Christian tradition were guilty of the ills of modern dispensationalism.[34] But it is precisely this connection that Middleton does not show. In fact, at this point his marshaling of arguments becomes problematic in multiple respects. While he does note that premodern millennial thought sometimes held out earthly hopes, he nowhere addresses how those earlier expressions relate to the present day (inasmuch as many, though not all, of these figures were what is now termed amillennialists). Further, he does assess

33. Richard John Neuhaus raised similar worries about the eschatology of N. T. Wright's *Surprised by Hope* in his *First Things* editorial of April 2008, to which Wright replied in a letter to the editor published in 2008.

34. Here is perhaps the greatest similarity to the arguments of Wright, in as much as both Middleton and Wright specifically note only errors found in recent theology influenced by modern dispensationalism but regularly shape their argument as responding to the wider catholic tradition.

that there was little discussion of the earthy nature of the final destiny of Christians (beyond the millennium), but the absence of evidence does not prove the absence of such belief. Finally, when he engages with secondary studies upon the nature of classical eschatology, he draws precisely the opposite lesson from what the text is conveying: when he quotes from Caroline Walker Bynum on how fifth-century Christians rarely "expected the millennial age to come soon," he takes this lessening of immediacy as evidence of a restriction of earthiness to the millennium rather than the final destiny, ignoring the immediately preceding line from Bynum that states that hopes for a new heaven and new earth "had not disappeared by the fifth century."[35] Simply put, his misuse of Levenson's (mentioned earlier) and now Walker Bynum's excellent studies does not bolster confidence in the historical accuracy of his charges of the widespread failure of the tradition. When Middleton turns to the hermeneutics and ethics of modern dispensationalism, he seems to be more adept in dealing with texts and marshaling evidence. But the argument that he and other Augustinian naturalists offer is marred when they tar and feather the classical tradition, accusing it of having lapsed into middle Platonic dualism. They assert that this decayed classical tradition influenced the catholic tradition without offering either textual evidence or nuanced analysis of how and where this diverged substantively from the teaching of the prophets.

There is also precious little engagement with Plato and the Platonic tradition in attempts at reforming biblical eschatology in a more earthy direction.[36] In a critique of N. T. Wright's holistic eschatology, Edward Adams observes:

35. Middleton, *A New Heaven and a New Earth*, 294, citing Caroline Walker Bynum, *The Resurrection of the Body in Western Christianity, 200–1336* (New York: Columbia University Press, 1995), 13.

36. By comparison, see the nuanced reflections of Mark DelCogliano, "Basil of Caesarea versus Eunomius of Cyzicus on the Nature of Time: A Patristic Reception of the Critique of Plato," *Vigiliae Christianae* 68, no. 5 (2014): 498–532.

It is somewhat ironic, given his keenness to dissociate ancient Jewish theology from Platonism, that in insisting on the incompatibility of the thought of the created cosmos coming to an end with Jewish creational monotheism, Wright himself exhibits a Platonic logic. For Plato, the demiurge was bound by his own nature to create an everlasting cosmos; a good god could not have done otherwise. By ascribing immortality and other perfections to the cosmos, Plato blurs the distinction between it and "god" (*Tim.* 34B; 68E; 92C). In Old Testament and early Jewish thought (generally speaking), there is more emphasis on the freedom and sovereignty of God vis-à-vis the created world. According to Ps. 102:25–27, the distinction between creator and creation is evident precisely in the fact that God is eternal, whereas heaven and earth will wear out and perish.[37]

Plato upheld the inviolability of the created order; the Bible raised metaphysical concerns about any such affirmation. While some middle Platonists veered in a different direction, the simplistic portraits presented by recent eschatological proposals regarding theology's fall into Platonic cosmology fail to accurately convey the philosophical parties in place, much less the judgments rendered by Hebrew prophets, intertestamental Jews, or apostolic writers. Again, these historiographic matters

37. Edward Adams, *The Stars Will Fall from Heaven: Cosmic Catastrophe in the New Testament and Its World*, Library of New Testament Studies 347 (London: T & T Clark, 2007), 253n1. Middleton addresses the slightly different emphases of his dialogues, with *Phaedo* being more radical and *Timaeus* presenting the earth as a reflection of heaven. But he summarizes, "nevertheless, the worldview that held together both versions of Plato's dualism, and that he bequeathed to later ages, involved the radically new assumption of an immortal, immaterial soul and the aspiration to transcend this present world of matter, sensation, and change in order to attain to a higher, divine reality" (*A New Heaven and a New Earth*, 31).

are significant in as much as Wright and Middleton position their arguments as rebukes to the mainstream catholic tradition, not simply to the narrow and recent niche of the Christian world that is influenced by modern dispensationalism.

Second, the Reformed tradition has always linked eschatological exposition with the question of covenantal and testamentary continuity. Middleton continues this hermeneutical maneuver, albeit with a twist. He notes that misperceptions creep in easily when one considers the apocalyptic proclamation of the apostolic witness apart from its background in the Old Testament writings. This caution is commendable, and neo-Marcionite hermeneutics is common enough today (typically under the guise of some "christocentrism") that it does not simply go without saying.

And yet Middleton never tracks in the other direction, following that great Augustinian dictum that the new is in the old concealed and that the old is in the new revealed. He only portrays a forward-moving hermeneutic without any suggestion that later redemptive acts might provide a new lens by which God's prior word might be better appreciated.[38] This hermeneutical narrowing has real implications: whereas John Calvin made a concerted effort to argue that the Israelites of the Old Covenant understood the spiritual significance of the covenantal blessings promised in the *torah*, Middleton argues exactly the opposite. He contends that the tangible and earthly character of those ancient promises finds its fulfillment in the New Testament witness.[39] Well, Calvin

38. On which see especially the writings of Richard Hays, *Echoes of Scripture in the Letters of Paul* (New Haven: Yale University Press, 1989); Richard Hays, *Reading Backwards: Figural Christology and the Fourfold Gospel Witness* (Waco, TX: Baylor University Press, 2014); Richard Hays, *Echoes of Scripture in the Gospels* (Waco, TX: Baylor University Press, 2016); in a slightly different register, see also Gregory K. Beale and Benjamin Gladd, *Hidden but Now Revealed: A Biblical Theology of Mystery* (Downers Grove, IL: IVP Academic, 2014).

39. Middleton, *A New Heaven and a New Earth*, 78, 95, 97, 105–7; cf. John Calvin, *Institutes of the Christian Religion*, 1:428–457 (II.x–II.xi.8).

would not deny that point: Abraham was promised some land in the Middle East. Eventually Jesus reiterates this by promising the meek the entire earth: a greatly extended plot of land, but a plot of land (and not an ethereal existence) just the same. Yet it was Calvin whose analysis of the law and gospel, the Old and New Covenants, was focused extensively on showing the unity of the testaments precisely by demonstrating that the patriarchs and other ancient saints did not long merely for earthly reward but for heavenly or spiritual blessings (as Calvin takes to be promised in the New Testament). Calvin posits no spiritualizing, as if physical blessings are exchanged for or only symbolic of spiritual rewards. But Calvin does consistently insist that physical blessings are symbolic of and secondary to the spiritual blessings of life with God.

We can celebrate Middleton's commitment—and that of other neo-Calvinists—to shape the material of our confession by not only the topics but even the scope and sequence of biblical attestation. Just as Katherine Sonderegger has recently prompted a rethinking for many regarding the way in which the Scriptures unfold the doctrine of God,[40] so we are reminded here that the doctrines of the covenant and of Christ must be unfurled in canonical sequence. However, honoring the flow of redemptive history does not mean that we trace only one thread—in this case, the earthy or material—through the narrative sequence. Calvin was attuned to canonical unity and to historical flow, yet he repeatedly emphasized and spent far more time in assessment of the heavenly attentiveness that is present even in the witness regarding Israel of old. Unless we discount the heavenly minded reading of those patriarchs given in Hebrews 11:13–16, we cannot reduce the confession of the prophets of old to that thin earthiness proferred by Middleton. We must instead offer a holistic vision that also takes in their spirit-minded faith that sought a "better

---

40. Katherine Sonderegger, *Systematic Theology*, vol. 1 of *Doctrine of God* (Minneapolis: Fortress, 2015).

country, that is, a heavenly one" (11:16). Given that only this hope led God not to be "ashamed to be called their God" (11:16), we do well not to miss the point.

Third, Middleton repeatedly notes that Christians regularly maintained hope in a bodily resurrection along with a heavenly destiny. He suggests this as a tension demonstrating a mental weakness or intellectual inability to allow the one to reconfigure the other. And yet his comments in this regard highlight another issue: the way in which theological systems and doctrinal distinctions function. Distinctions are made not to box in ideas and allow us to pick and choose from seemingly divergent notions. Rather, distinctions function to keep us, as theologians, alert to all that Holy Scripture reveals, lest we give in to our deep inclinations to narrow our focus upon some hobby horse, some familiar territory, or some comfortable concept.

The church's affirmation has always included confession that Jesus Christ will return to judge the living and the dead, "and his kingdom will have no end," as well as that we look forward to "the resurrection of the body and the life everlasting." These creedal statements signal facets of our hope; they are not options from which we choose but aspects that we must simultaneously affirm. The tension expressed in much exposition of Scripture between earthy reality and heavenly destiny mirrors the tension of Scripture: the glorified body of our Lord was creaturely, finite, accessible to sight and touch, and yet it passed through walls. While the resurrected character points to the continuity of final life with this present world, the heavenly aspect of that same life reminds us that a great transformation awaits, one that cannot be fully fathomed this side of the irrupting light of the returning Christ.[41]

41. Middleton's book includes no reference to the teaching of Matthew 22:30, namely, that in our resurrected life we will be like the angels rather than giving ourselves in marriage to one another. His emphasis on our earthly vocation (even in the eschaton) is helpful, but his silence regarding this remarkable teaching skews his portrait away from its spiritual center,

In another register, W. D. Davies and Dale Allison remind us that the Bible presents texts that speak of God as incapable of being seen and others that suggest that God will finally be visible in the eschaton. The truth, of course, is found not in negotiating some proximate medium between the two but in discerning the mysterious truth signaled by the distinct contribution of each text in its own integrity.[42] We will return to this concern in the next chapter, as we seek to reform the classical approach to the beatific vision in a Christ-centered key that befits the broader patterns of Trinitarian being and action.

Appreciating and affirming tensions of imagery do not constitute a liability in theological work. Far from it. The rational tensions of biblical imagery are signs of the fullness of God's revelation. In this case, we do well to theologize in such a way that we can sing not only the breadth but also the depths and emphases of Charles Wesley's remarkable words in "Love Divine, All Loves Excelling":

> Finish then thy new creation; pure and spotless let us be;
> let us see thy great salvation perfectly restored in thee:
> changed from glory into glory, till in heaven we take our
>   place,
> till we cast our crowns before thee, lost in wonder, love,
>   and praise.

Here a place taken "in heaven" does not undercut the reality of "thy new creation"; the heavenly nature of the new creation finds explanation in the very presence of the triune God ("before thee"). The new creation and the restored world are diverse images,

---

that is, that we will be wed to Christ and, thus, no longer need the symbol of human matrimony.

42. W. D. Davies and Dale Allison, *A Critical and Exegetical Commentary on the Gospel according to Saint Matthew*, International Critical Commentary (Edinburgh: T & T Clark, 1988), 1:457.

which the prophets and the apostles pull together in varied ways to attest to the reality that God's apocalyptic action will be novel and interruptive, and not just the next step in the forward march of human history. It is also a word of hope for this world in its own given nature rather than a different plan yet to be hatched—an eschatological audible that might somehow signal God's intent to replace this world with another. That pairing of images ought to be matched alongside another: the evangelical hope that we shall dwell in the new heavens and new earth as well as the joyous anticipation of heaven. While they are not the same image, they are overlapping—not juxtaposed or contradictory—portraits. Indeed, the newness of that creation hearkens ultimately to its heavenly character, for it is God's presence that renders it new, peaceful, and beautiful.

Fourth, the shift toward eschatological naturalism relates to emphases regarding Christian ministry and witness and of ecclesiastical identity in the Reformed tradition. George Marsden identified three major streams within the Reformed ecclesiastical world in North America: the doctrinal, the pietist, and the culturalist.[43] Marsden noted that these were ideal types, and none likely existed apart from the others. But we ought to note that they have sometimes functioned as party types, as if the whole ecclesial body might be made up of persons or congregations marked particularly by one of them. And we ought to note that the culturalists predate the Kuyperian or neo-Calvinist movement; in fact, Marsden notes that this type dates back before the nineteenth century.[44] However, it has been the work of Kuyperians to provide the intellectual framework and, in many cases, the institutional forms for that culturalist development in the twentieth and twenty-first centuries.

43. George Marsden, "Introduction: Reformed and American," in *Reformed Theology in America: A History of Its Modern Development*, ed. George Marsden (Grand Rapids: Baker, 1997), 3.
44. Marsden, "Introduction: Reformed and American," 6.

These types all hearken back to facets of the catholic and Reformed faith. They cannot be parties, nor can they be causes—not without significant loss. The tendency of neo-Calvinism to lapse into eschatological naturalism ought to prompt us to remember the heritage of the *nadere reformatie* in the Dutch Reformed church or the heritage of the combination of pietism with cultural reflection so evident in the practical divinity of the English Puritans. And, of course, that heritage, which is so prominent in those two streams of the Reformed tradition, finds its roots deeper, not only in the springs of reformational figures like Bucer, Calvin, Cranmer, or Luther, but also in the patristic and medieval testimony of Basil and of Augustine, of Gregory and of Bernard. While the "culturalist" or "transformationalist" emphasis has been powerfully rediscovered in the neo-Calvinism of the Reformed world, we do well to keep an eye always on the catholic faith: all that has been attested by all Christians at all times. In particular, we should note the tendency of neo-Calvinist hope to lapse into naturalist concern for cultural perfection.[45] Rooted deep in the Reformed tradition itself, the pietist emphasis upon communion with God can continue to serve as both a salve and a prompt for that terrible fissure. May it be so, for we want never to think of the eschaton apart from theology.

We have noted that reforms can have either a productive or parasitic effect. While the Kuyperian and neo-Calvinist reforms can take and have, at times, taken a parasitic turn in modern eschatology, taking the form of what can only be called eschatological naturalism, these eschatological reforms regarding the earthiness of Christ's kingdom and Christian hope can and should be held with greater regard among a wider catholic audience so that they are productive and helpful to Christian witness and to the

---

45. Parallel warnings have been issued by Timothy J. Keller, "What Is So Great about the PCA?" (June 2010), 14. Available online: http://barkerpro ductions.net/what_pca.pdf (accessed October 24, 2017).

ongoing task of biblical exegesis and proclamation. In this case, we need to retrieve the catholic substance of the Christian faith within which recent reforms regarding its earthiness can serve a productive rather than a parasitic role. In other words, the order of the day must be to locate an earthy eschatology within a much deeper emphasis upon a truly and functionally theological eschatology so that God remains not only the instrument and guarantor but the personal center and very substance of our hope. In remembering the earthiness of the kingdom, may we never forget its heavenliness as well, that is, that the kingdom is defined, first and foremost, by the presence of the King of kings and Lord of lords: "Behold, the dwelling place of God is with man" (Rev 21:3).

2

The Visibility of the Invisible God

Reforming the Beatific Hope

A survey of the vast terrain of modern Protestant divinity evidences a deep abyss: the doctrine of the beatific vision has dropped into oblivion. Friedrich Schleiermacher affirms the doctrine—albeit with great uncertainty about how it can be conceptualized (as either a static perfection of our God-consciousness or as a progressively advancing yet never hindered experience of that God-consciousness)—within the space of one page and touches upon it nowhere else.[1] When we survey twentieth-century Protestant theology, we see that Schleiermacher's successors paid less attention to this doctrine than he. A glance through the index to or the text of Karl Barth's *Church Dogmatics* fails to register reference to this doctrine. Emil Brunner, his contemporary, offers a paragraph's worth of analysis to the promise that "We shall see God face to face."[2] Hans Schwarz

---

1. Friedrich Schleiermacher, *The Christian Faith*, ed. H. R. Mackintosh and J. S. Stewart (Philadelphia: Fortress, 1976), 719–20.
2. Emil Brunner, *The Christian Doctrine of the Church, Faith, and the Consummation*, vol. 3 of *Dogmatics*, trans. David Cairns and T. H. L. Parker (Philadelphia: Westminster, 1962), 440.

This chapter was previously published in Michael Allen, "The Visibility of the Invisible God," *Journal of Reformed Theology* 9, no. 3 (2015): 249–69.

offers no attention to the topic in his essay on eschatology in the influential, Lutheran *Christian Dogmatics* textbook edited by Carl Braaten and Robert Jenson, and that extended essay's silence is matched in his monograph on eschatology as well.[3] As for Robert Jenson, he concludes volume 2 of his *Systematic Theology*, which is titled *The Works of God*, with a chapter entitled "Telos." Therein he offers a compact and revisionist approach to the beatific vision in the course of one sentence: "God will let the redeemed see him: the Father by the Spirit will make Christ's eyes their eyes." The revisionist character of this claim—merging Christ and the redeemed—is clarified by one more sentence: "Under all rubrics, the redeemed will be appropriated to God's own being."[4] Gerhard Sauter never mentions the topic in his *What Dare We Hope? Reconsidering Eschatology.*[5] The two most acclaimed German-language systematic theologies of the latter twentieth century are par for the course. Jürgen Moltmann's *The Coming of God* mentions the *visio Dei* in three brief places: in one short sentence ("when he appears we—and they—will see him as he is and be like him [1 John 3:2]"), another phrase ("before his 'revealed face'"), and finally in another sentence ("we shall be able to look upon his face without perishing").[6] And Wolfhart Pannenberg only mentions the notion in passing when describing how Benedict XII opened the door in the fourteenth century

---

3. Hans Schwarz, "Eschatology," in *Christian Dogmatics*, ed. Carl Braaten and Robert Jenson (Minneapolis: Fortress, 1984), 2:475–588; Hans Schwarz, *Eschatology* (Grand Rapids: Eerdmans, 2000).

4. Robert W. Jenson, *Systematic Theology*, vol. 2 of *The Works of God* (New York: Oxford University Press, 1999), 369.

5. Gerhard Sauter, *What Dare We Hope? Reconsidering Eschatology* (Harrisburg, PA: Trinity Press International, 1999). One sentence of this text (on 107) addresses the "vision of God," but it refers to God's vision of us (which, we are told, reconfigures how we see ourselves), not our own vision of God.

6. Jürgen Moltmann, *The Coming of God: Christian Eschatology*, trans. Margaret Kohl (Minneapolis; Fortress, 1996), 107, 296, 317.

to thinking that the intermediate state held all salvific privileges within it (including the beatific vision).[7]

While eschatology has moved front and center in twentieth-century Protestant theology, the beatific vision appears to have exited stage right.[8] The absence is glaring in the face of the substantial place that the doctrine of the beatific vision held in classical faith and practice, where the beatific vision played a role in prolegomena (as the ultimate form of human knowledge of God), in eschatology (as the central hope of the Christian), and in ethics (as the driving force or motivation for ascetic discipline). Roman Catholic theology in the modern era has continued to attend to this classical locus, ranging from consideration in papal encyclicals to dogmatic textbooks to the historical and philosophical studies that have marked its most vibrant conversations in recent decades. Indeed it has remained tethered to discussions of nature and grace, and it has appeared in the arguments by and against the so-called *nouvelle théologie* that so dominated the middle and later twentieth century.

Modern Protestant divinity, however, has only rarely engaged the topic and typically only in very abbreviated analyses. There are reasons—polemical in nature—for this absence. Perhaps an example is instructive in helping to unpack them. Herman Bavinck offers lengthy comment upon eschatology in his *Reformed Dogmatics*, taking in topics of the intermediate state, the return of Christ, chiliasm, Israel's future, the day of the Lord and judgment, and the renewal of creation.[9] Yet the notion of

7. Wolfhart Pannenberg, *Systematic Theology*, trans. Geoffrey Bromiley (Grand Rapids: Eerdmans, 1998), 3:577. He also offers an oblique reference to how the phrase "entering into" in Matthew 5:8 likely refers to the vision of God (528n7).

8. A notable exception is the recent account offered by Anthony C. Thiselton, *Life after Death: A New Approach to the Last Things* (Grand Rapids: Eerdmans, 2012), 185–215.

9. Herman Bavinck, *Holy Spirit, Church, and New Creation*, vol. 4 of *Reformed Dogmatics*, ed. John Bolt, trans. John Vriend (Grand Rapids: Baker

the beatific vision receives less than two paragraphs of attention (722). Bavinck's focus is upon the dangers of spiritualism. He admits that "present in the New Testament there is undoubtedly some spiritualization of Old Testament prophecy," noting the ways in which the double appearance of Christ requires some of his kingdom's characteristics to be true for a while only spiritually and then, upon his return, physically as well. "But this does not confine this blessedness to heaven. This cannot be the case as is basically evident from the fact that the New Testament teaches the incarnation of the Word and the physical resurrection of Christ; it further expects his physical return at the end of time and immediately thereafter has in view the physical resurrection of all human beings, especially that of believers" (718). His assessment: "All this spells the collapse of spiritualism." Indeed, "as misguided as it is—along with pagan peoples and some chiliasts—to make the material into the chief component of future blessedness, so it is also one-sided and stoic to regard the physical indifferently or to exclude it totally from the state of blessedness" (720). Bavinck views this as a uniquely Protestant emphasis upon the renewal of creation; monasticism having symbolized the Eastern and Roman focus upon a purely supernatural hope that he terms "abstract" and "exclusively transcendent." In summary he notes that "the Reformation, going back to Scripture, in principle overcame this supernaturalistic and ascetic view of life" (721).

Bavinck does affirm the vision of God as part of his discussion of the "blessings of the redeemed." "Contemplation (*visio*), understanding (*comprehensio*), and enjoyment of God (*fruitio Dei*) make up the essence of our future blessedness. The redeemed see God" (722). A heightened notion of this vision is offered: it is enjoyed "directly, immediately, unambiguously, and purely" as is appropriate to an image of God's own knowledge of himself. Bavinck

---

Academic, 2008), 589–730. Future references to this work are noted in the text by page numbers in parentheses.

turns then to debates among medieval theologians regarding the seat of this vision of God: whether in the mind (Thomas) or the will (Scotus) or some combination thereof (Bonaventure). The exposition does not offer a particular approach to this question, nor does it even express why it mattered or from where its positions were coming. But it is acknowledged nonetheless.

What do we make of theology done where the beatific vision ceases to have any real sway or force? Whether in Bavinck's minimal attention or in the complete absence of any focus as found in others, we cannot deny that the topic has failed to capture either the scrutiny or imagination of modern Protestant theologians. We might shift our question ever so slightly: what losses occur, systematically, when this locus ceases to function in an operative manner? We might analyze those losses in two categories: direct losses and indirect losses. In both cases it ought to be noted that these losses are not necessarily true in every case of one who denies or displaces the beatific vision. They are, rather, likely symptoms that can be systematically traced out by reflecting on the function played by this doctrine in classical divinity and, thus, noting what doctrinal atrophy may well or may likely set in when one substantial piece of the gospel puzzle is pulled out.

Directly, the absence of the beatific vision from modern Protestant divinity leads to a particular lacuna within the world of Christian eschatology. Surely it will be unlikely to fall into spiritualism, as feared by Bavinck, but it could run the risk of some form of naturalism. Perhaps it will not be a strictly immanentist naturalism, bereft of divine involvement or gracious enablement, but it may well be a naturalism nonetheless. Eschatology may turn to focus upon the renewal of creation by means of articulating the ways in which society, selves, and structures are restored to their created ends. Particularly in efforts to think beyond spiritualization of the faith or in apologetic concern to relate to broader anthropological projects of great value, eschatology can be related primarily to this-worldly states of affairs. Spiritualism is not the only reductive game in town.

Indirectly, however, there could be potential for a number of related losses caused by the receding role, if any, played by the beatific vision in modern Protestant divinity. At least two major concerns come to the fore immediately. First, a loss of focus upon the beatific vision can skew a Christian account of humanity by foreclosing or, worse yet, dismissing a constituent facet of human teleology. A recent volume by Hans Boersma, *Heavenly Participation*, attempts to articulate and counter this tendency in modern eschatology.[10] Similarly one of Matthew Levering's major objections to the eschatology of N. T. Wright and other New Testament scholars involves the way in which concern about supernaturalistic approaches can quickly become myopic and lose sight of the transcendent presence of the triune God who will be with his children and visible to them.[11] Boersma and Levering present a theocentric vision of humanity—such that it would be false to construe their concerns as narrowly anthropological—nonetheless their attention is fixed firmly upon anthropological questions viewed in light of the story and promises of Jesus Christ. Anthropological missteps have been noted when the beatific vision is either sidelined or dismissed, and suggested recalibrations that claim to be better attuned to the Platonist-Christian synthesis or the Thomistic tradition are put forward as a better way.

A second formal loss occurs, however, when the beatific vision ceases to have an operative role in thinking about Christian faith and practice. We must not only ask about how this absence will affect our anthropology but also attend to how it will shape

10. Hans Boersma, *Heavenly Participation: The Weaving of a Sacramental Tapestry* (Grand Rapids: Eerdmans, 2011).

11. Matthew Levering, *Jesus and the Demise of Death: Resurrection, Afterlife, and the Fate of the Christian* (Waco, TX: Baylor University Press, 2012), 109–26.

our theology proper. Specifically, what does the beatific vision tell us about God? We are inquiring not about humanity and our end but about God and his purposes: in what ways has the beatific vision enriched and underwritten a particular view of God's character and will, and in what ways will its absence or recession likely recast that understanding of God's character?

This chapter will attempt to address these questions by turning to one modern Protestant theologian who did address the beatific vision at length, G. C. Berkouwer. In his account of the *visio Dei*, Berkouwer related this doctrinal locus to the divine attributes, specifically to the question of divine invisibility. He offered what can safely be called a fairly iconoclastic account of the divine character, suggesting that the reality of our hope in the *visio Dei* ought to have led theologians to deny the doctrine of invisibility. In our considerations, then, we will address this question regarding the potential theological impact that the beatific vision might have regarding the (in)visibility of the triune God. Our analysis will trace four steps. First, we will consider the roots of the doctrine of divine invisibility within the classical theological tradition. Berkouwer charges the doctrine as an accretion from Greek philosophy, so its roots in biblical and/or philosophical analyses must be assessed. Second, we should turn to the biblical promise of the beatific vision and the ways in which its scriptural exposition touches upon the divine character, asking if the prophetic and apostolic witness suggests that a connection like the one articulated by Berkouwer ought to be articulated herein. Third, we will unpack the Trinitarian shape of God's (in)visibility, asking if these are shared attributes or are characteristics proper to one or more of the divine persons. Fourth, then, we will be in a position to reflect upon the claims that God is invisible and visible, their theological merits, and their synthetic relations. In so doing, hopefully, the significance of retrieving the classical focus upon a theocentric notion of beatitude will be matched with an equally vital commitment within Reformed theology to further aligning that beatific vision along Christ-centered and specifically Trinitarian lines.

Whence Invisibility?
The Exegetical Roots of the Classical Affirmation

Almost unique among modern dogmaticians in the Protestant world, G. C. Berkouwer offers a spacious account of the *visio Dei* in his extended study *The Return of Christ*.[12] Indeed this chapter and that volume serve as an illustrative microcosm of his dogmatic project: patiently assessing the biblical witness, charitably journeying through the various historical debates, and passionately engaging contemporary concerns and questions. Berkouwer's Studies in Dogmatics series always showed a concern to renew the theological practice of the church by retrieval from the past: both from the scriptural witness of the prophets and apostles and their intellectual and spiritual reception in the history of the catholic church. In this instance, however, Berkouwer's engagement of the tradition winds up taking an element of that catholic tradition (the focus upon the beatific vision and its relation to various theophanies) and suggesting that it requires modification of another facet of that tradition (the doctrine of divine invisibility). What unfolds as a process of traditioning shows itself, in this instance, to be a practice of decidedly critical traditioning.

G. C. Berkouwer's notable attention to the *visio Dei* leads him to affirm the visibility of God and, in so doing, to deny the invisibility of God as a divine attribute. He suggests that the doctrine of invisibility has a problematic source and a failed ability to make sense of the breadth of biblical teaching, specifically of texts that

12. G. C. Berkouwer, "*Visio Dei*," in *The Return of Christ*, ed. Marlin van Elderen, trans. James van Oosterom, Studies in Dogmatics (Grand Rapids: Eerdmans, 1972), 359–86. Future references to this work are noted in the text by page numbers in parentheses.

address the sight of God. Berkouwer is not unaware of texts that suggest God cannot be seen. He can note a litany of such biblical teachings:

> The Old Testament tells us that no one can see God and live (Exod 33:20); John goes further: "no one has ever (*pōpote*) seen God" (John 1:18; cf. 1 John 4:12); and Paul takes it to the ultimate: "no man has ever seen or can see" God (1 Tim 6:16). It is as if invisibility is an indubitable attribute of God (cf. 1 Tim 1:17). (360)

It would be more accurate, he says, to consider these limits of permission, not capacity: God may not be seen, not God cannot be seen. "There are passages in the Bible where seeing God is spoken of as a deadly danger. Obviously, it is not at all a dogmatized 'invisibility' that accounts for this, but the very possibility of seeing him"; he presses still further: "The *possibility* of seeing God is the background of the fear of the consequences" (361). Berkouwer suggests that limits are moral, not optical, and relate to permission, not capacity.

If not from these texts, where does Berkouwer see invisibility coming into the history of doctrine? According to his historical assessment, it is here that we see an instance of hellenization and of overreaction to Greek thought. On the one hand, he suggests that a paucity of references to the vision of God may be a strong reaction to the Greek focus upon "beholding" that he believes is part of that mentality (360). On the other hand, several times throughout his chapter Berkouwer suggests that the development of the doctrine of the beatific vision was owing to Greek influence of various sorts. He cites E. Baert's argument that "because of the influence of Hellenistic mysticism and Greek appreciation for contemplation, later theology placed greater influence on seeing God than did the NT" (360n1). He later notes, in connection with the development of invisibility as a Christian doctrine, Rudolf

Bultmann's comparison of Greek and Israelite-Jewish religion, suggesting that the latter does not include any notion of invisibility and, by implication, that later patristic reflections in this vein must be influenced by Hellenistic sources (364n11). Later he comes back to Bultmann's claim that *aōratos theós* (language of "the invisibility of God" as found in Colossians 1:15, 1 Timothy 1:15, and Hebrews 11:27) arose "in connection with other Hellenistic divine predications" (367n18). Finally, when he discusses the medieval claim that the beatific vision actually involves sight of God's essence (*per essentiam*), he notes Herman Bavinck's argument that this betrays the influence of neo-Platonic mysticism (374).

Berkouwer is not making these doctrinal claims in his own voice. In each and every case he is making reference to the reception-historical and comparative religious analyses of other scholars: Baert, Bultmann, and Bavinck. Two things remain noteworthy, however, in assessing these citations. First, it is not atypical for Berkouwer to make claims in a third-person voice; the breadth of his dogmatic survey in this Studies in Dogmatics series means that he often speaks through the voice of various experts, be they biblical scholars or historians of philosophy and of dogma. Second, it is worth noting that he nowhere shows any pause, hesitation, or disagreement with any of these historical judgments. While he is more than willing to critique various critics throughout his volumes, here he only notes them affirmatively and, we must assume, with agreement. Thus, we are led to conclude that the overwhelming suggestion of Berkouwer is that the apostolic writings of the New Testament betrayed a relative disinterest or lack of emphasis upon the beatific vision as an intentional contrast with contemporary Hellenistic thought, but that later Christian theology developed this focus on the *visio Dei* because it had been influenced by that same Hellenism. Paul Gavrilyuk's language, developed in his study of the doctrine of impassibility, is illuminating here as well, for Berkouwer surely presents a sketch of "theology's fall into Hellenistic philosophy," at least with respect to the doctrine of divine invisibility.[13]

Berkouwer is surely right to note that invisibility has been treated as if it were "an indubitable attribute of God." He notes that the confession of his own church, the Belgic Confession, affirms invisibility alongside a host of other classical attributes of God: "We all believe with the heart, and confess with the mouth, that there is one only simple and spiritual Being, which we call God; and that he is eternal, incomprehensible, invisible, immutable, infinite, almighty, perfectly wise, just, good, and the overflowing fountain of all good."[14] Invisibility is nothing unique to the Reformed confessional or dogmatic tradition. It is a staple in classical Christian divinity. Exegeses and homilies related to John 4:24 ("God is spirit") or Colossians 1:15 ("the image of the invisible God") were regularly invoking the language of invisibility by patristic, medieval, and Reformation-era theologians.

Questions might be raised, however, about Berkouwer's historical judgments. First, the suggestion that Greek influence lies behind this affirmation raises as many questions as it answers. Which Greek tradition does he suggest exercises such influence? Does it do so uncritically? While he is willing to note that Greeks were a "people of the eye," we might press further and ask why this Greek thought would lead Christians to speak of God as invisible. Specificity must be sought. Second, we ought to inquire

13. Paul L. Gavrilyuk, *The Suffering of the Impassible God: The Dialectics of Patristic Thought*, Oxford Early Christian Studies (Oxford: Oxford University Press, 2006).

14. "The Belgic Confession (1561, Revised 1619)," in *Reformed Confessions of the Sixteenth Century*, ed. Arthur Cochrane (Louisville: Westminster John Knox, 2003), 189 (article 1). Similar language is found in the Second Helvetic Confession ("Second Helvetic Confession [1566]," in *Reformed Confessions of the Sixteenth Century*, 228 [chapter 3]) and the Westminster Confession of Faith ("Westminster Confession of Faith," in *Creeds of the Churches: A Reader in Christian Doctrine from the Bible to the Present*, ed. John H. Leith, 3rd ed. [Louisville: John Knox, 1982], 197 [chapter 2]).

after biblical texts that exceed the exegetical parameters of Berkouwer's own account, for some texts do not seem to tie invisibility to moral concerns but to ontological limits.

We will not offer a full taxonomy of ways in which Greeks thought about divine (in)visibility, nor a genealogical account of how this myriad of approaches were received critically and, perhaps, uncritically by various figures within the early Christian churches. We do not foreclose such discussion or suggest that it is uninteresting, though its resolution will not be our present concern. Suffice it to say, though, that the question of biblical exegesis sufficiently provokes reconsideration of Berkouwer's approach on its own terms. It need not be shown that no "Greek mentality" influenced him one way or another to appreciate the wider biblical pressure toward the doctrine of divine invisibility as found in not only the Reformed but also the deeper catholic tradition of theological reflection. For instance, Wolfgang Musculus not only affirms the invisibility of God but also praises certain pagan thinkers for their awareness of this divine attribute: Pythagoras, Cato, Virgil among them. But Musculus is not thereby claiming to have developed his theology of divine invisibility out of this pagan context; rather, he is noting a shared belief that he has found explicitly confessed in texts like John 4:24.[15] Appreciating Musculus as one conversant with—and not always dismissive of—pagan philosophy while also motivated and pressured by biblical exegesis does not, of course, prove that neither he nor any other Christian theologian has ever been influenced deleteriously by extra-biblical notions of invisibility. But it does put the lie to the notion that this must be the case and

15. Wolfgang Musculus, *Loci communes sacrae theologiae*, 3rd ed. (Basel: Johann Herwagen, 1573), I.iii; Wolfgang Musculus, *Commonplaces of Christian Religion* (London: R. Wolfe, 1563), 8. See Richard A. Muller, *Post-Reformation Reformed Dogmatics: The Rise and Development of Reformed Orthodoxy, ca. 1520 to ca. 1725*, vol. 3 of *The Divine Essence and Attributes* (Grand Rapids: Baker Academic, 2003), 299.

prompt a critically yet sympathetically engaged assessment of the history of doctrine.[16]

The Belgic Confession lists Romans 1:20 for its claim that invisibility rates among the other divine attributes. This passage is notably absent from Berkouwer's chapter on the *visio Dei*, even though it is the one and only explicit biblical citation for this doctrinal affirmation in his church's confessional standards. In that passage Paul writes: "For what can be known about God is plain to them, because God has shown it to them. For his invisible attributes, namely, his eternal power and divine nature, have been clearly perceived, ever since the creation of the world, in the things that have been perceived" (Rom 1:19–20 ESV). Ambrosiaster commented: "God, who is invisible by nature, in order to be knowable to visible creatures, made a work which in its own visibility revealed its maker."[17] What is remarkable about this text—and Berkouwer's silence regarding it—is the fact that Paul is working here with the doctrine of creation and revelation prior to the entrance of sin and affirming God's invisibility as a reality that shapes our relationship to God prior to our moral failings. Romans 1:20 does not speak of divine permission or lack thereof for sight of God. It speaks of inability to experience sight of God in those who are (at that time) morally upright.

16. It is worth noting that awareness of God's visibility is not a novelty in the supposedly post-metaphysical era or in a time dominated by narrative theology. Quite the contrary, these various biblical instances of divine visibility have been debated through the centuries. For example, seventeenth-century "Anthropomorphites" and the scholastics of the high period of Reformed Orthodoxy debated their meaning, not their existence (see Muller, *Post-Reformation Reformed Dogmatics*, 3:303–7). While invisibility texts may receive less attention by post-metaphysical theologians, it is false to reverse that statement and suggest that divine visibility texts were somehow less noted or even discussed by those theologians who worked within the parameters of what goes by the name of classical theism.

17. Cited in Peter Lombard, *The Sentences*, vol. 1, *The Mystery of the Trinity*, trans. Giulio Silano, Mediaeval Sources in Translation 42 (Toronto: Pontifical Institute of Mediaeval Studies, 2007), 19 (distinction 3, chapter 1).

While Berkouwer may well be right that some biblical texts only mention God's not being visible as a moral limit (not an optical or ontological restriction), the biblical witness does include texts that seem to speak in that broader metaphysical manner. Romans 1:20—along with other texts such as Colossians 1:15 and 1 Timothy 1:17—seems to speak of invisibility as a divine attribute and not simply the way in which God is experienced now by sinners incapable of "seeing him who is invisible" (Heb 11:27). And even though some fascination with and expression of the nature of the beatific vision may be owing to the influence of certain bits of Greek thought, Christian theologians from the classical and reformational traditions have seen fit to note both sources in pagan philosophy and the prophetic and apostolic writings of Holy Scripture, to differentiate the two, and to root their own claims authoritatively in the latter.

When Visibility?
The Eschatological Promise of Divine Sight

We have seen that the doctrine of divine invisibility has a biblical pedigree, so that Berkouwer's claim that it is merely a Hellenistic accretion cannot be sustained. Again, it may have been heightened or even altered by Hellenistic thought, but it is not a mere positing of Greek philosophy alone: biblical exegesis of a slew of texts guided its transmission and development. That said, we must attend now to another strand of texts in the Holy Scriptures that address God's visibility. In particular, we must reflect on the theological implications of the beatific vision.

The beatific vision does not appear out of nowhere, canonically speaking, but comes amidst a narrative wherein God is occasionally "seen." Genesis 3:8 recounts the walking of God in the garden of Eden, suggesting that he was ocularly available for engagement by Adam and Eve. Interpreters have regularly read the appearance of the visitors to Abraham in Genesis 18 as a theophany in as much as they take first-person speech upon their lips and identify it as divine. Jacob wrestles with the Almighty, as recounted in Genesis 32. Moses sees the back side of God around the cleft of a rock: it is not the sight of God requested, but it is nonetheless a positive bestowal as described in Exodus 34. Later sensory experiences are recounted at various points in the Old Testament (1 Kgs 22:19; Isa 6:1).

These attestations of divine sight are regular enough that we find a stock reference arise in the psalms of Israel regarding the expectation and experience of divine sight (e.g., 11:7; 17:15; 27:4; 34:8, 12; 36:9; 123:2).[18] Eventually the psalmist knows enough to ask the necessary question: "When shall I come and behold the face of God?" (Ps 42:2). Such a query only makes sense amidst an ongoing tradition wherein God is believed to be visible and intimately so (visible in the face itself). As Psalm 11:7 states, there are moral conditions to such beholding: "For the LORD is righteous; he loves righteous deeds; the upright shall behold his face." But for those who are righteous, this blessed vision forms a part of their promised reward, even if their present experience (oftentimes calamitous and persecuted) suggests otherwise.

And, of course, such references are not limited to the Old Testament, as if the New Testament does not describe any visual experience of God. Far from it, for the Apocalypse of Jesus Christ as revealed to John on Patmos culminates not simply with a promise of the new heavens and new earth or the heavenly Jerusalem but with the vision of God, for "they will see his face" (Rev 22:4). Apostolic writings match this apocalyptic vision, for Paul speaks consistently of the coming vision of God in Christ (e.g., 1 Cor 13:12; 2 Cor 3:17–18). Here the promised beatific vision

18. For argument regarding this metaphorical yet literal speech about God, see Patrick D. Miller, *The Lord of the Psalms* (Louisville: Westminster John Knox, 2013), 29–38.

finds expression in the psalms of David, in the prophetic witness of the exiled people of God, and in the apostolic and apocalyptic eschatology of the nascent Christian church.

Jesus himself points forward to this blessed hope: "Blessed are the pure in heart, for they shall see God" (Matt 5:8). His words, however, do note that such a reality is a blessing and, as such, is reserved for those who are clean. It is not a naturally available experience, much less something that can be coerced or manipulated via technological, moral, relational, or phenomenological tinkering. It remains a blessing invoked by its object and no one else. He calls such blessed hope into existence; we do not summon it. And his blessed vision is attained by the "pure in heart." This moral contingency is noted in other writings of the New Testament. "Strive for peace with everyone, and for the holiness without which no one will see the Lord" (Heb 12:14).

Visibility is nowhere portrayed as an easily accessed thing. On the one hand God is not typically available in this time. He has prepared his disciples—and through their apostolic witness, the church at large—for his perceived absence or, perhaps better put, presence in a different way. He will now be present through the witness of his Holy Spirit (John 13:19, 26; 16:4–15). On the other hand, even God's breaking in—whether in the form of a temporary theophany or the enduring incarnation of the Son—is not accessible to all. Many observe without seeing. Some saw his miracles and faithfulness and did not believe; some saw all this and more and executed him. And this is not a novelty in the New Testament. Indeed, "the notion of incarnation only makes sense in the New Testament if it reflects, points to, or arises out of what we know about God in the Old Testament."[19] So the presence of God is palpable in both testaments, but in neither case do we find that all who come within eyesight of God are aware of his appearance.

19. Miller, *Lord of the Psalms*, 31.

74

The prophets and apostles witness to the presence of God, and their testimony to this reality takes the form of ocular language of beholding God. At various high points in the divine economy we see that God is made visible to his people: in Eden, upon Sinai, in the temple, and during the ministry of Jesus. Further, we see that there is a strong and growing sense that implicit in our blessed hope is a beatific vision, namely, that God will be fully and finally visible to his people. This glorified vision contrasts with the perceptional absence of God and the limited and qualified vision experienced even in notable moments of his history of revelation. Thus, our dogmatic reflections upon the theological implications of the beatific vision must attend to the link between the biblical witness to the visibility and the invisibility of the triune God.

Whose Visibility? Reformed and Catholic Specifications on Trinitarian Visibility

Before fully diving into the question of addressing how visibility and invisibility relate in the triune life, we do well to attend to one common way of proceeding. It is not abnormal to construe the Trinity as fundamentally invisible (as Spirit) and to view divine visibility as entirely a function of the incarnation of the divine Son. Thus, the Son is confessed as visible (in his humanity) while the Father and the Holy Spirit are nonetheless fully invisible. We do well to note the appeal of such a schematic. It allows for two bifurcations. First, there is a Trinitarian bifurcation wherein visibility only ever occurs in the case of the Son upon his incarnation. Second, there is a theological bifurcation between the invisibility of God and the visibility of the Son's humanity.

The apostolic witnesses to the incarnation do mark it as a unique and startling occurrence. The Johannine Prologue is exemplary, though not unique, in this regard. "No one had ever seen

God; the only God, who is at the Father's side, he has made him known" (1:18). While there had been theophanies and prophetic visions beforehand, there is something new here. So new that Paul can speak to the Ephesians and Colossians about a mystery that has only now been revealed and make use of language of darkness and light to express this newfound clarity and manifestation in Christ Jesus (Eph 1:9; Col 1:26–27; 4:3). In light of this apostolic emphasis we must ask a series of questions: is divine visibility located only here? and, in its presence here, is it only visibility of the Son? and, still further, is it truly visibility only of his human nature? These questions deserve consideration.

First, it is necessary to note that both the incarnation and the event of Pentecost involve divine visibility in some fashion. Whether in the arms of Mary or atop the heads of the early disciples, sight conveys divine action and genuine divine presence in power. Pentecost, of course, is not the only occurrence of pneumatological visibility. One cannot but remember the dove-like descent at the occasion of Jesus's baptism in the Jordan River. In neither case does the Spirit become manifest in something that is an enduring form; yet in both cases the Spirit does reveal himself to us in, with, and through visible media.

Thomas Aquinas reflected upon such occurrences in his discussion of what he terms "visible missions." In the midst of his discussion of the Trinity in the *Prima Pars* of the *Summa theologiae*, he concludes by addressing the missions of the persons in question 43. Missions are occasions wherein the movement of the divine life stretches out beyond God's own internal life to engage others; here processions take shape as external missions in relating to others. In article 7, Thomas poses the question "whether it belongs to the Holy Spirit to be sent visibly." He first notes false paths: seeming theophanies, prophetic visions, and the sacraments of the Old and New Testaments are not occasions wherein any visible mission occurs. Yet Thomas does note two instances where a visible mission is expressed: the baptism of Jesus and the day of Pentecost.[20] Thomas does not conflate these missions with that of the Son's incarnation; of them he says: "The Holy Spirit, however, did not take up the visible creatures in which he appeared into a unity of person in such a way that what is ascribable to them could be applied to him."[21] The Spirit does not continue to have any relationship to a dove or a tongue of fire, and the Spirit never enjoyed a hypostatic union with either one. They are visible missions nonetheless. Thus we confess that visible missions are not all of a sort in as much as the Son does continue to exist as Jesus of Nazareth and does enjoy a hypostatic union of divine and human natures while other visible missions do not continue to exist.[22]

Second, the New Testament witness points to the Christological nature of the beatific vision. "For God, who said, 'Let light shine out of darkness,' has shone in our hearts to give the light of the knowledge of the glory of God in the face of Jesus Christ" (2 Cor 4:6). Indeed, the apostles witness not only to the positive promise of sight of God in Christ but also to the exclusion of any other sight of God the Father. "Not that anyone has seen the Father except he who is from God; he has seen the Father" (John 6:46). There is one way who brings truth and life (John 14:6); he is the only vision we have of the Father. This is at the heart of not only Johannine but all apostolic theology: "And the Word became flesh and dwelt among us, and we have seen his glory, glory as of the only Son from the Father, full of grace and truth" (John 1:14).

---

20. Thomas Aquinas, *Summa theologiae*, Ia, Q. 43, Art. 7, *ad* 2.

21. Thomas, *Summa theologiae*, Ia, Q.43, Art. 7, *ad* 1.

22. Cyril distinguishes between seeing the divine essence (what he terms "the nature of God in its very substance") and what Ezekiel identifies as "the appearance of the likeness of the glory of the Lord" (Ezek 1:28). "More precisely, it was a likeness that conveys God-befitting thoughts like a picture, while the truth of these matters surpasses mind and speech" (Cyril of Alexandria, *Commentary on John*, ed. Joel Elowsky, trans. David Maxwell, Ancient Christian Texts [Downers Grove, IL: IVP Academic, 2013], 1:70 [on John 1:18]).

The beatific vision of the incarnate Son is possible, fully and finally, because God in his freedom has assumed human form and, implied therein, has assumed a human nature. This external act, however, takes Trinitarian form. The Son's incarnational manifestation before the world stage is not a solo performance. Though he is the only one who assumes human form and takes on a human nature, he does so by the Spirit's power (as confessed in the creeds and attested by the Gospels) and at the Father's will (as he so frequently reminds us in his own words in the Gospels). That baptismal account visibly attests this differentiated harmony: the Father speaking of his will and pleasure, the Spirit descending to anoint with power, and the Son as the center and focus of attention as God's Beloved. The Son and the Spirit alike are visibly involved in manifesting God's mission to the world, but these are not separable, much less competing, missions. The external works of the Trinity are undivided, though they are differentiated.

So we must first observe that while the incarnation is the moment where God becomes definitively visible, this does not mean that only the Son acts visibly to reveal God. In the baptismal account and then in the day of Pentecost, the Spirit's mission takes visible form as well. And the Son's own manifestation is a Trinitarian—and not only a Christological—act. It is the result of the concerted will of the full triune God: Father, Son, and Holy Spirit. We must now turn to the second question, regarding whether or not the incarnational visibility of the Son is restricted to his humanity or also involves his divinity or his person. In this regard we will listen not only to the patristic witness and that of Thomas Aquinas but also to John Owen and the developing tradition of Reformed Christology.

It is not a *novum* in the Reformed tradition or the work of John Owen to suggest that it is the humanity of the divine Son that enables vision of God. Indeed, Gregory of Nyssa offers a reading of the Song of Songs 1:16 that renders the notion of "thick shading" (*suskios*) as an identification of the humanity of the Son that enables vision of God's face.[23] Hans Boersma comments that "Gregory here describes the human nature of Christ as a bodily garment (*peribole*) that overshadows his divinity, so that the Incarnation not only permits the divine nature to be present in and with the human nature but also allows us to see the very Son of God."[24]

Yet the attendant condition of the humanity of Christ does not mean that the blessed vision of God in the face of Christ can be reduced to a vision of his humanity. Rather, we see him: the person of the Son of God, "God of God, Light of Light, Very God of Very God." Just as the person is the subject of all incarnational action, so the person is the object of all beatific vision. We might break this down grammatically. The Son as Son is visible. But the Son as Son is visible by means of his humanity. Here Owen and the Reformed tradition are affirming with Augustine that the humanity of the Son is the instrument by which the vision of God occurs. Yet they are also going beyond Augustine. Michel René Barnes has described how Augustine insisted that the visions of God in the Scriptures (whether theophanies in the Old Testament era or the incarnation in the New Testament) were occasions of "created matter being used as an instrument of communication by the Trinity" and, indeed, that "what is seen is not God; it is a sign or symbol of God's presence."[25] Augustine believed Matthew 5:8—the beatitude noting that the pure in heart (and they only) will see God—located any actual sight of God at the eschaton and not before. Augustine believed our sight was restricted to the humanity of Jesus, a sign of God that is itself (as a human nature) not God.

23. Gregory of Nyssa, *In canticum canticorum* 4.107.9–108.12.

24. Hans Boersma, *Embodiment and Virtue in Gregory of Nyssa: An Anagogical Approach*, Oxford Early Christian Studies (Oxford: Oxford University Press, 2013), 91.

25. Michel René Barnes, "The Visible Christ and the Invisible Trinity: Mt. 5:8 in Augustine's Trinitarian Theology of 400," *Modern Theology* 19, no. 3 (2003): 346.

Herein lies the contribution of Reformed Christology, as best expressed by Owen, in maintaining the emphasis upon the particular humanity of the Son as the place wherein God is seen and at the same time insisting (beyond even Augustine) that *God* really is seen here. Further, this has eschatological implications: Jesus really has brought forward the kingdom and, in his person and presence, given us a foretaste (not a substitute) of the eschatological hope to which we journey in faith. That is, we see *God* and not simply an instrument of or attachment to God in this vision. Reformed Christology in Owen's vein really does note that his human nature makes actual such sight, rendering it in the categories of the eye and the senses. But it is equally insistent, notably so when viewed against its Augustinian backdrop, that in seeing according to the humanity one really is seeing God's Son, the second person of the Trinity. As Gregory's description suggests, the humanity of the Son is the garment giving form to this vision, but it is the *person* in the garment who we see: the divine Son.

The words of the Johannine Prologue are pertinent again: "And the Word became flesh and dwelt among us, and we have seen his glory, glory as of the only Son from the Father, full of grace and truth" (John 1:14). The incarnate Word who tabernacles among us brings visibility not merely to a man named Jesus, but specifically to "his glory," that is, "glory as of the only Son from the Father." The reference to the unique (*monogenēs*) Son surely must refer to the divine Son as person as opposed to referring to the human nature of Jesus alone. John does not merely say this one dwelt among us; he uses the term for the tabernacle presence of God in the Old Covenant, *eskēnōsen*. Jesus's dwelling is God's dwelling. That this is so can be seen from the next phrase, wherein his singular sonship is marked out by his being "full of grace and truth." This phraseology is derived, most likely, from the words of the text of Exodus 34, wherein God's name was proclaimed before Moses atop Mount

Sinai.[26] If John has identified the Son with YHWH by way of one of the great theophanies of the Old Testament as well as the ongoing glory present in the tabernacle, then our vision is not simply of the human Jesus, but in the human Jesus we really do see God.

The visible mission of the Son is just that: a visible mission of the Son. Personal visibility occurs only through the instrument of Jesus's humanity, no doubt, but this tabernacle really does serve as a "garment" in which the person of the Son—the unique, divine Son—is made manifest to us. Reformed theologians like John Owen have emphasized, therefore, not only the necessity of Christ's human nature for making God personally visible but also that in so doing Christ's human nature really does make the Son of God *personally* visible. In so doing, they affirmed Augustine's argument but extended it further (with Gregory of Nyssa) to emphasize the genuine sight of God himself in the incarnation.

Dogmatics and Dialectics: The Image of the Invisible God

One might think that we have run our course, then, by offering an anatomy of the beatific vision and by addressing its economic and incarnational shape through reflection on the Christological focus and Trinitarian context of the apostolic promise of this *visio Dei*. But we do well to press further into Trinitarian theology without allowing fear of speculation to preclude raising questions of deeper immanent import. We may find that we cannot resolve or answer all such questions. Nonetheless, we do well to ask what deep truths regarding the immanent processions and the intrinsic fullness and glory of the triune life are expressed in the particular

26. See D. A. Carson, *The Gospel according to John* (Grand Rapids: Eerdmans, 1991), 129–30. Carson traces the terminology of Exodus 34:6–7 (*hesed* and *'emet*) through the Old Testament, Septuagint, and into intertestamental Judaism.

course of these visible divine missions. Specifically, what truths are conveyed in the visibility of the Godhead that is expressed in the face of Jesus Christ and attested to by the empowering given by his Holy Spirit.

That we ought to press further is impelled by the fact that the external works of the Trinity are indeed undivided. While only the Son was made incarnate, this occurred by the Holy Spirit and at the Father's behest. The whole Trinity willed this effect and worked to this end. Thus, while only one person was hypostatically visible, we must say that the whole Trinity wills and works divine visibility. Appropriations language may well prove most appropriate in describing this ergonomic harmony: the Father works visibility by his loving and expressive will, the Son works visibility by his receptivity toward the triune prompting and the flesh prepared by the Spirit, and the Spirit works visibility by bringing the love of the Father into the truthful face of the Son's appearance. Our previous exploration of how Christological specificity relates to full triune involvement must impel us, then, to affirm that the whole Godhead is marked by an attribute of expression.[27] According to the Father's will, in the Son's face, and by the Spirit's power, the triune God images forth his invisibility.

That such questions are worth exploring is signaled further by the fact that the Son is not merely visible. Indeed, according to diverse strands of the patristic consensus regarding Christological and Trinitarian orthodoxy, the Son remained invisible as well. Michel René Barnes has traced a developing consensus among pro-Nicenes that whether in the East (Origen) or West (Hilary of

27. Visibility need not be the only such mechanism linguistically for affirming this "attribute of expression": divine speech and aural metaphors may be employed (as by many today who make much of speech act theory's helpfulness and its roots in triune discourse: e.g., Kevin Vanhoozer). A wider biblical idiom, of course, is the very notion of glory, which can refer not only to weightiness *in se* but also to *gravitas* amongst others (which is based on weightiness *in se* but only comes into being as such when extended amongst others).

Poitiers and later Augustine), the Son was confessed to be—and, more specifically, to continue to be—both visible and invisible after the assumption of a human nature. Indeed a large part of Augustine's polemic against the Homoians involved argument that the Son was invisible, in as much as the Homoians believed invisibility was a defining attribute of the Godhead.[28] And Thomas Aquinas also raised the question of whether invisible grace—the fruit of the invisible mission(s) of the Trinity—includes what we must call an invisible mission of the Son as well as the Spirit. Thomas affirmed such, arguing in *Summa theologiae* Ia.43.5 that the entire Trinity works sanctifying grace in God's people so that both the Word (the Son) and Love (the Spirit) come to dwell within them invisibly. Here the patristic witness and its reception in at least one great master of medieval scholasticism, Thomas Aquinas, not only affirm that the Son was invisible in eternity and in the immanent life of God but also that the Son acts invisibly in the divine missions and in the triune God's life with us.

So the whole Godhead moves to express its glory outward and even the most visible of the persons—the incarnate Son—continues to possess the attribute of invisibility. We do well, then, to speak of the visibility of the invisible God and to insist on maintaining that entire confession. Claims about the inner life of God seem apposite here. Cyril of Alexandria claims that "the divine nature sees and is seen in a way that is fitting to God."[29] The shared glory of the three divine persons befits only God, but this Trinity of love and light does share this inner-Trinitarian visibil-

28. Barnes, "The Visible Christ and the Invisible Trinity," 335 (on Augustine's argument against the Homoians). This insistence that the Son—even after the time of the incarnation—remains invisible serves as a doctrinal precursor to the *extra Calvinisticum* made famous in early Reformed Christology. On the catholic roots of that doctrine, see E. David Willis, *Calvin's Catholic Christology: The Function of the So-Called* Extra Calvinisticum *in Calvin's Theology*, Studies in Medieval and Reformation Thought 2 (Leiden: E. J. Brill, 1966), 29–60.

29. Cyril of Alexandria, *Commentary on John* 155 (on John 1:18).

ity. Without bringing creatures to share in this natural knowledge and sight, the loving Lord of eternity does elect that creatures participate in this light and wisdom by grace and according to their creaturely capacity. Our vision of God is not the same as God's own vision, but it is remarkably real nonetheless.

By way of conclusion, I offer a prompt for further analysis. In respect of another divine attribute (impassibility), Paul Gavrilyuk has offered reflection upon Cyril's teaching regarding the character of the eternal God, the expression of and experience of suffering in the life of the incarnate Son, and the link between the two. In so doing he has argued that a particular patristic dialectic was maintained in the exegetical and dogmatic reflections of Cyril, namely, that we must speak of the suffering of the impassible (non-suffering) God.[30] In his argument he showed that "divine impassibility is primarily a metaphysical term, marking God's unlikeness to everything in the created order, not a psychological term denoting (as modern passibilists allege) God's emotional apathy."[31] God is emotionally involved in relations with the world, yet these are metaphysically distinct from the ways in which creatures engage other creatures (psychologically). Further, "the intent of the paradoxical statements is to hold God's transcendence and undiminished divinity in tension with the divine care for creation and involvement in suffering."[32]

---

30. Gavrilyuk, *The Suffering of the Impassible God*; see also Paul Gavrilyuk, "God's Impassible Suffering in the Flesh: The Promise of Paradoxical Christology," in *Divine Impassibility and the Mystery of Human Suffering*, ed. James F. Keating and Thomas Joseph White (Grand Rapids: Eerdmans, 2009), 127–49. Other parallels could be found with the historical analysis of Gregory of Nyssa's theology of ascent in both his *Life of Moses* and *Song of Songs* in Nathan Eubank, "Ineffably Effable: The Pinnacle of Mystical Ascent in Gregory of Nyssa's *De vita Moysis*," *International Journal of Systematic Theology* 16, no. 1 (2014): 25–41.

31. Gavrilyuk, "God's Impassible Suffering in the Flesh," 139.

32. Gavrilyuk, "God's Impassible Suffering in the Flesh," 148.

The biblical witness and its doctrinal development in the catholic and Reformed tradition suggest that we ought to speak of the visibility of the invisible God. God's invisibility is not merely a statement regarding his ocular presence but a metaphysical marker that denotes his ontological distinction from all things visible and invisible. Not only that, but we can extend beyond Gavrilyuk's immediate point. Such a marker (this dialectic of the visibility of the invisible God) points not only to God's transcendence but to his triunity and to the reality that God sees God and any other sight is by gracious participation and bestowal of that sight to someone who does not possess that life in himself or herself. God is no thing. God is seen by God. That God can be seen by any thing, any created kind, any human—this is miracle, and this is grace by way of participation. God is visible. God remains invisible. In the gospel, these startling and seemingly paradoxical claims are affirmed together. Hymnody expresses this most potently:

> Immortal, invisible, God only wise,
> In light inaccessible, now hid from our eyes,
> Most blessed, most glorious, the Ancient of Days,
> Almighty, victorious, thy great name we praise.[33]

The invisible God remains inaccessible even in his light. The point of the paradoxical pairings is to keep the freedom and the love of God before us and, in so doing, to remind ourselves of the remarkable gospel promise that the very God who cannot be seen reveals himself to us in the face of Jesus: he is the "image of the invisible God" (Col 1:15). Hence Reformed theologians (such as Owen and Edwards) have agreed with Gregory of Nyssa that we will not see the divine essence but will see God by means of theophanic (and

33. Walter Chalmers Smith, "Immortal, Invisible, God Only Wise," in *Trinity Hymnal* (Suwanee, GA: Great Commission Publications, 1990), 38.

specifically Christophanic) disclosure.[34] The paradoxical language of the invisible making himself visible points, therefore, also to the particularity of that manifestation in Christ.

The silence of modern Protestant divinity regarding the doctrine of the beatific vision may render us susceptible to tone-deafness when it comes to the words of Jesus's promise that if we have seen him, we have seen his Father (John 14:9). Further, it may lessen our grasp of the deep reality underneath that promise, namely, that this triune God determines to be seen by those who do not enjoy his eternally full divine sight on their own. "God's goodness is a communicative, spreading goodness. . . . If God had not a communicative, spreading goodness, he would never have created the world. The Father, Son and Holy Ghost were happy in themselves and enjoyed one another before the world was. But that God delights to communicate and spread his goodness, there had never been a creation nor a redemption."[35] Richard Sibbes attests to this reality—God's triune fullness and his eternally loving bent toward sharing that goodness with others—and it can be related directly to sight, for the Scriptures tell us that goodness and flourishing are found only in God's presence. "You make

---

34. Hans Boersma has been researching the development of this strand of reflection from Nyssa in the East to Owen and Edwards in the Reformed realm. See "The 'Grand Medium': An Edwardsean Modification of Thomas Aquinas on the Beatific Vision," *Modern Theology* 33, no. 2 (2016): 187–212; Hans Boersma, "Becoming Human in the Face of God: Gregory of Nyssa's Unending Search for the Beatific Vision," *International Journal of Systematic Theology* 17, no. 2 (2015): 131–51; Hans Boersma, *Seeing God: The Beatific Vision in Christian Tradition* (Grand Rapids: Eerdmans, 2018); see also Suzanne McDonald, "Beholding the Glory of God in the Face of Jesus Christ: John Owen and the 'Reforming' of the Beatific Vision," in *The Ashgate Research Companion to John Owen's Theology*, ed. Kelly Kapic and Mark Jones (Aldershot: Ashgate, 2012); a contrarian account has been offered by Simon Gaine, "Thomas Aquinas and John Owen on the Beatific Vision: A Reply to Suzanne McDonald," *New Blackfriars* 97 (July 2016): 432–46.

35. Richard Sibbes, "The Successful Seeker," in *The Works of Richard Sibbes*, vol. 6 (Edinburgh: Banner of Truth Trust, 1983), 113.

known to me the path of life: in your presence is fullness of joy; at your right hand are pleasures forevermore" (Ps 16:11). One of the great glories of the gospel—central to its promise of human flourishing upon the bestowal of the fullness of Christ's grace—is the pledge that the invisible God makes himself visible to us.

3

Heavenly-Mindedness

Retrieving the Ascetical Way of Life with God

Friedrich Nietzsche viewed Christianity as suspect, not least for what he deemed its "slave ethic." He believed a philosophy ought to encourage first self-empowerment and then also self-expression; Christianity's religious approach, in contrast, seemed an unacceptable restraint on the modern spirit. Language of service, discipleship, obedience, law, and the like suggested narrow conformity and a debased, subservient posture.[1] Nietzsche's take has been widely influential, and in this era divine rule is read as human repression. In particular, Nietzsche's heirs have seen Christianity's heavenly focus as a distraction or opiate: focusing upward, on the mythic heavens, we acquiesce to our miserable earthly plight. The spiritual, then, preserves the material status quo. The ethereal props up earthy injustices and frustrations.

Nietzsche's influence has been wide enough that even the audience of C. S. Lewis's *Mere Christianity* needed to be addressed along these lines.

1. Friedrich Nietzsche, *Jenseits von Gut und Böse: Zur Genealogie der Moral*, Nietzsche Werke: Kritische Gesamtausgabe 6.2, ed. Giorgio Colli and Mazzino Montinari (Berlin: De Gruyter, 1968), 218–35.

A continual looking forward to the eternal world is not (as some modern people think) a form of escapism or wishful thinking, but one of the things a Christian is meant to do. It does not mean that we are to leave the present world as it is. If you read history you will find that the Christians who did most for the present world were just those who thought most of the next. The Apostles themselves, who set on foot the conversion of the Roman Empire, the great men who built up the Middle Ages, the English Evangelicals who abolished the Slave Trade, all left their mark on Earth, precisely because their minds were occupied with Heaven. It is since Christians have largely ceased to think of the other world that they have become so ineffective in this. Aim at Heaven and you will get earth "thrown in": aim at earth and you will get neither. [2]

The Oxford don knows that modern people worry that a focus upon eternity actually amounts to "a form of escapism." His reply deserves our attention. Not only atheistic folk like Marx but also Lewis's thinly religious audience in mid-twentieth-century Britain had imbibed a good dose of Nietzsche's criticism.

A cynical approach to heaven is not required, however. In recent years, D. A. Carson has pointed to the prayers of Paul as an exemplar of the Christian way. In a set of lectures now published under the title *Praying with Paul*, Carson offers exposition of several prayers found in the Pauline epistles (2 Thess 1:3–12; 1 Thess 3:9–13; Col 1:9–14; Phil 1:9–11; Eph 1:15–23; Rom 15:14–33). [3] While each chapter warrants unique attention, readers are alerted quickly to a common theme and emphasis. Car-

2. C. S. Lewis, *Mere Christianity* (New York: HarperOne, 2015), 135.
3. D. A. Carson, *Praying with Paul: A Call to Spiritual Reformation*, 2nd ed. (Grand Rapids: Baker Academic, 2015).

son shows the notably spiritual inflection of Paul's concerns. While Paul would address some very earthy situations, he did so with a spiritual lens and theological focus, addressing spiritual realities and needs more than common concerns or comforts. Paul's prayers manifest the pattern called for by his Lord and our Savior: "Seek first the kingdom of God and his righteousness, and all these things will be added to you" (Matt 6:33). Whenever I have observed or participated in a conversation about this pervasive theme in Carson's book, readers have invariably sensed that it undermines legitimate concern for earthly matters (not only their own but those of their neighbors, indeed, of the whole world).

Theology not only seeks guidance or answers regarding the questions we bring to the table but all the more to find our very questions reshaped by God's revealed instruction. In this chapter, we want to show how the heavenly-mindedness that so marked the prayers of Paul and the kingdom priorities espoused by Jesus himself can reframe the way in which we consider Christianity this side of Nietzsche, Marx, and the materialism of the modern era. Building on the exegetical work of earlier Christians, we will seek to show some connections between elements of the gospel and this heavenward focus and spiritual lens. While such synthetic analysis may not convince the modern masters of suspicion, we may nonetheless appreciate the way in which a heavenly tilt invigorates a genuine humanism rather than leading to its undoing. In that regard, we hope to make good on the apt suggestions of Lewis by showing how heavenly-mindedness is part of the very warp and woof of Christian discipleship, not some mere appendage. We do well to retrieve the heavenly imagination for our contemporary Christian vocations.

Preliminaries

Two preliminary matters deserve attention. First, this chapter was almost titled "Spiritual-Mindedness." We do well to attend to and meditate upon all things spiritual. We must contemplate God in and of himself, for he is the font of all blessing and gifts in his gospel. His perfect life is the root of all our sustenance as it was the source of our very creation. But we must also speak of "heavenly-mindedness," for the Bible calls us not simply to God but to the God who has turned toward us and pledged himself to us in the gospel. The language of "heaven" speaks to God's special presence amidst creation, for heaven is a created realm permeated with and defined by his very presence and rule. Over against earth per se, heaven represents that space and time whereby God has provided and guided. And yet heaven can also be contrasted with the purely spiritual, for it involves not only the divine life but also that eternal reality turned unto the creaturely realm in grace and mercy. So we rightly speak of heavenly-mindedness in as much as we contemplate not only the one true God of the Trinity but also the way in which this God has freely willed to be with us in Christ and not apart from us.[4]

Second, we have to face head-on the fact that the heavenly focus of Paul's prayers may seem decidedly alien to us in our secular or materialistic world. The secular age is not so much an age of ardent denial of the divine as it is a time bereft of spiritual concern. Charles Taylor has used the language of the "immanent frame" to portray the limited lens through which secularly shaped moderns imagine self and world.[5] James K. A. Smith has tried to

4. Just as speaking of God's ubiquity flows from his immensity within the triune life but extends that omnipresence in his operative works amongst the created order.

5. Charles Taylor, *A Secular Age* (Cambridge, MA: Belknap Press of Harvard University Press, 2007). Taylor's arguments in this massive tome were suggested briefly in his lecture "A Catholic Modernity?," in *A Catholic Mo-*

draw out Taylor's analysis to note ways in which even the ardently religious are secularized. Smith's diagnosis is stark as he speaks of an "eclipse of heaven" and a focus upon ends that are material and earthy, not spiritual or transcendent. Notice that, in so doing, he does not address ills outside the church, or even maladies marking the revisionist churches, or skeptical or nominal Christians, only in ecclesiastical or sociological terms. Rather, he says: "So even our theism becomes humanized, immanentized, and the telos of God's providential concern is circumscribed within immanence. And this becomes true even of 'orthodox' folk: 'even people who held to orthodox beliefs were influenced by this humanizing trend; frequently the transcendent dimension of their faith became less central.' Because eternity is eclipsed, the this-worldly is amplified and threatens to swallow all."[6] Not just Marxists or ideologues who follow Nietzsche overtly but also dutiful members ensconced in the rolls of the baptized need to hear Lewis speak of the humane implications of the call to heavenly-mindedness, because Babylon has found a way to shape even the formation of the children of Zion.

Ethics and prayer are the obvious registers for such dissonance. Whereas classical Christianity has followed Paul in focusing on the eternal and the spiritual, modern secularism's immanent frame has shifted even Christian action and prayer ever toward a focus on material concerns and earthy blessings. People may take a more or less conservative or liberal/progressive tack in approaching such issues, be they economic, social, and cultural, or perhaps psychological, physiological, and financial. More often than not, such binaries are less than helpful in clarifying the desires, intentions, and actions of real men and women, much less

dernity? Charles Taylor's Marianist Award Lecture, with Responses by William Shea, Rosemary Luling Haughton, George Marsden, and Jean Bethke Elshtain, ed. James L. Heft (New York: Oxford University Press, 1999), 16.

6. James K. A. Smith, *How (Not) to Be Secular: Reading Charles Taylor* (Grand Rapids: Eerdmans, 2014), 49–50.

the cries of their voiced prayer unto the Lord. But the tilt toward the mundane and the earthy in even our most pious moments, our stated and spontaneous instances of prayer, conveys a notable sign that we are schooled to be out of step with the biblical impulses of classical Christianity. Even many taught not to embrace the prosperity gospel are no less inundated with earthy concerns. If we were to truly inventory our prayers of thanksgiving and of supplication, or the dominant questions and themes of theological inquiry, we would find this to be the case. The sense of shock when people read Carson's study of Paul's prayers highlights this chasm powerfully, and the analysis of Taylor and Smith helps make sense of the history of our cultural (mal)formation in this regard.

The Grace and Duty of Spiritual-Mindedness

We begin by casting our earthiness into sharp relief by turning to a classic divine whose emphases and order help demonstrate the contingency of our contemporary fascinations.

We do well to glean from the order and passion of John Owen's classic account entitled "The Grace and Duty of Being Spiritually Minded."[7] In that text Owen attests to the significance of the spiritual and the way in which the God who is Spirit himself had turned, in grace and of his freedom, to bless us with all that which he possesses in and of himself. Out of his fullness he has filled us (Eph 1:23). Because he fills us, we are called to find our very being and our every blessing where he is, in the heavens (Rom 8:6; Col 3:1).

Owen observed "the present importunity of the world to impose itself on the minds of men, and the various ways of insinu-

7. John Owen, "The Grace and Duty of Being Spiritually Minded," in *Sin and Grace*, ed. William T. Goold, Works of John Owen 7 (Edinburgh: Banner of Truth Trust, 1965), 263–497. Future references to this work are noted in the text by page numbers in parentheses.

ation whereby it possesseth and filleth them" (263–64). Whereas Paul commended God's being as that from whom all are filled (Eph 1:23; 3:19), Owen saw a climate whereby the world insinuates its capacity to fill or satisfy. In speaking of imposition and even importunity, Owen speaks to its pressure (especially subliminally). The claims of the world, however, do not sit well with our design, so the words of Paul remind us that only the spiritually minded experience life and peace (Rom 8:6). Owen begins by speaking to the necessity of this mind-set: "To be spiritually minded is the great distinguishing character of true believers from all unregenerate persons." Indeed, "where any are spiritually minded, there, and there alone, is life and peace" (271). His text traces out the nature of this celestial claim upon our minds and our very lives.

What does it mean to be spiritually minded? What particular duty is conveyed by Paul in Romans 8:6?

> Three things may be distinguished in the great duty of being spiritually minded:
> 1. The actual exercise of the mind, in its thoughts, meditations, and desires, about things spiritual and heavenly;
> 2. The inclination, disposition, and frame of the mind, in all its affections, whereby it adheres and cleaves unto spiritual things;
> 3. A complacency of mind, from that gust, relish, and savour, which it finds in spiritual things, from their suitableness unto its constitution, inclinations, and desires. (270)

Owen views thoughts as manifesting and molding affections. "Ordinarily voluntary thoughts are the best measure and indication of the frame of our minds" (275; where he is drawing on Ps. 23:7). Thus, a first evidence of being spiritually minded comes when one's inward promptings are unto heavenly realities, occurring when suggested not only by external forces but also by personal intuition. When one intuitively turns to heavenly matters, then one has internalized heavenly affections in a significant way. "The second evidence that our thoughts of spiritual things do proceed from an internal fountain of sanctified light and affections, or that they are acts or fruits of our being spiritually minded, is, that they abound in us, that our minds are filled with them" (298). To gauge the intuitiveness and extent of spiritual-mindedness, he suggests that Psalm 119 may be used as a canon for self-examination (301). In so doing, the Puritan divine suggests that we look not only to see thoughts or meditations but also joyous delights so to assess their spiritual caliber. Affection, not mere thought, is the aim whereby life and peace are enjoyed in Christ.

To sum up thus far, "Spiritual affections, whereby the soul adheres unto spiritual things, taking in such a savour and relish of them as wherein it finds rest and satisfaction, is the peculiar spring and substance of our being spiritually minded" (395). We are not left to this duty alone, but God commits himself to our cause as Father and Redeemer. So Owen then says: "I shall consider and propose some of those arguments and motives which God is pleased to make use of to call off our affections from the desirable things of this world" (397). Before spiritual-mindedness is duty, it is grace.

Six facets of divine beneficence receive exposition.

> First, he hath, in all manner of instances, poured contempt on the things of this world, in comparison of things spiritual and heavenly. . . . Secondly, God hath added unto their vanity by shortening the lives of men, reducing their continuance in this world unto so short and uncertain a season as it is impossible they should take any solid satisfaction in what they enjoy here below. . . . Thirdly, God hath openly and fully declared the danger that is in these things, as unto their enjoyment and use. . . . Fourthly, things are so ordered in the holy, wise

dispensation of God's providence, that it requires much spiritual wisdom to distinguish between the use and the abuse of these things, between a lawful care about them and an inordinate cleaving unto them. . . . Fifthly, God makes a hedge against the excess of the affections of men rational and, any way enlightened unto the things of this world, by suffering the generality of men to carry the use of them, and to be carried by the abuse of them, into actings so filthy, so abominable, so ridiculous, as reason itself cannot but abhor. . . . Lastly, to close this matter, and to show us what we are to expect in case we set our affections on things here below, and they have thereby a predominant interest in our hearts, God hath positively determined and declared that if it be so, he will have nothing to do with us, nor will accept of those affections which we pretend we can and do spare with him and spiritual things. (397–410)

"As unto the principle acting in them, that our affections may be spiritual and the spring of our being spiritually minded, it is required that they be changed, renewed, and inlaid with grace, spiritual and supernatural" (411). Expounding Paul's teaching that sanctification is unto the "whole Spirit, soul, and body" (1 Thess 5:23), Owen seeks to distinguish and thus highlight the breadth and variety of grace given to draw us from the darkness into God's glorious light. Grace is the principle, so that God's action serves as the ontological and ethical prompt. Various verbs are employed to speak of the gravity of this divine action: "changed, renewed, and inlaid." And the character of the grace inlaid is confessed to be both "spiritual and supernatural," and Owen notes that we are beyond the need for mere physical supplement or mental reorientation. We demand a truly transformative and renovatory work—resurrection, mind you—of our very affections. A root canal is necessary rather than a mere crown placed atop the moral or spiritual status quo.

This "spiritual and supernatural" prompt really does intrude to form "our affections" so that we really do exist and act as human subjects. Owen calls his readers to consider God and all things in God. His account of God's grace and our duty to be spiritually minded should be read alongside his other text, "Meditations and Discourses on the Glory of Christ, in His Person, Office, and Grace: With the Differences between Faith and Sight; Applied unto the Use of Them That Believe."[8] A Christological inflection flavors that treatise, although both texts point to meditation upon the glory of God in and of himself (in his person), in his works (in his . . . office), and of his benefits ("in his . . . Grace"). Indeed, the span of spiritual-mindedness flows epistemologically from its ontological character, for Owen elsewhere notes that our benefits are all enjoyed by way of beholding him: "For if our future blessedness shall consist in being where he is, and beholding of his glory, what better preparation can there be for it than in a constant previous contemplation of that glory in the revelation that is made in the Gospel, unto this very end, that by a view of it we may be gradually transformed into the same glory."[9] Being spiritually minded and viewing the glorious Christ is not to be myopic, then, but to view all things in a transfigured light. It is no narrow icon but the discipline of having one's whole imagination recast.

This vision of Owen has not dominated the modern spiritual imagination, however, for Nietzsche seems to have had a greater impact even among those who persist in faith and reli-

8. Owen, "Meditations and Discourses on the Glory of Christ, in His Person, Office, and Grace: With the Differences between Faith and Sight; Applied unto the Use of Them That Believe," in *The Glory of Christ*, ed. W. Goold, Works of John Owen 1 (Edinburgh: Banner of Truth Trust, 1955), 273–415. For a helpful sketch of his christologically inflected account of not only meditation but also the beatific vision, see Suzanne McDonald, "Beholding the Glory of God in the Face of Jesus Christ: John Owen and the 'Reforming' of the Beatific Vision," in *The Ashgate Research Companion to John Owen's Theology*, ed. Kelly Kapic and Mark Jones (Aldershot: Ashgate, 2012), 141–58.

9. Owen, "The Glory of Christ," 274.

gious commitment. For the modern, the Christian life dare not be thought apart from the various entanglements of human life: embodiment, ethnicity, gender, economic class, or sociopolitical and educational demographics. Each lens adds a seemingly illumining frame to the way in which recent theological work has focused upon questions of praxis. Spawned by many impulses, such concerns help provoke significant and, in many cases, overdue reflection on the place of grace in the midst of everyday realities. Shirley Guthrie has rightly pointed to the earthy frame of Christian spirituality:

> Any spirituality, including supposedly Christian spirituality, that retreats from the world into the self-serving piety of a private religious life is a false spirituality that flees rather than seeks God. True Christian spirituality cheerfully and confidently plunges into the life of our dirty, sinful, confused world, for there is where we meet the Spirit of the triune God who is present and at work not to save people from but in and for the sake of that world—the world that was and is and will be God's world.[10]

The significance of families, kingdoms, and lands in the stories of the Old Testament reminds us that divine presence and power come amidst the full and tangible lives we live and see around us. Far as the curse is found (Gen 3:14–19), so far runs the span of redemption (see esp. Ezek 36–37).[11]

10. Shirley Guthrie, *Always Being Reformed: Faith for a Fragmented World* (Louisville: Westminster John Knox, 1986), 86. See also the emphasis on the mundane in Janet Martin Soskice, *The Kindness of God: Metaphor, Gender, and Religious Language* (Oxford: Oxford University Press, 2007), esp. 7–35, 157–80.

11. On the breadth of Old Testament eschatological hope with Ezekiel 36–37 as a heuristic lens, see Donald E. Gowan, *Eschatology in the Old Testament* (Edinburgh: T & T Clark, 1999).

And yet one must wonder if a sense of theological priority and proportion might be in danger of being lost. While it is vital to see the social aspects of gospel concern and of Christian integrity, we do well to remember the way in which biblical teaching regarding Christian discipleship actually unfolds. How much of our religious practice and theological discussion goes on without demanding anything specifically Christian? To what extent does talk of hope, in particular, simply affirm that Christians too can hope for and work unto the same desires and yearnings of others, whether drawn from a particular sociopolitical program or ethnocultural identity?[12] Thankfully common grace reminds us that we can link arms with our neighbors regarding many civic projects, moral visions, and other concerns. Yet we do well to ask where Christian light must nonetheless name and address worldly darkness (John 1:9).[13] As we seek to own up to living hope, we must offer not merely a theology that piles on where others have stood but a genuinely "theological theology" that first attests "the way, the truth, and the life" that is irreducibly tied to the name of Jesus (John 14:6).[14] To that end, we must not only speak of earthly

12. See the commentary regarding the public, intellectual witness of Cornel West over against Marilynne Robinson in this regard in Alan Jacobs, "The Watchmen: What Became of the Christian Intellectuals?," *Harper's* (September 2016): http://harpers.org/archive/2016/09/the-watchmen/.

13. On the common propensity to critique the Johannine dualism of light and darkness due to the liberal project of pluralism in the realm of political philosophy and for a generative response, see Miroslav Volf, "Johannine Dualism and Contemporary Pluralism," in *The Gospel of John and Christian Theology*, ed. Richard Bauckham and Carl Mosser (Grand Rapids: Eerdmans, 2008), 19–50; see also Robert H. Gundry, *Jesus the Word according to John the Sectarian: A Paleofundamentalist Manifesto for Contemporary Evangelicalism, Especially Its Elites, in North America* (Grand Rapids: Eerdmans, 2002), esp. 51–70, 103–4, 108–14.

14. John Webster, "Theological Theology," in *Confessing God: Essays in Christian Dogmatics II* (London: T & T Clark, 2005), 11–31; see also Michael Allen, "Toward Theological Theology: Tracing the Methodological Principles of John Webster," *Themelios* 41, no. 2 (2016): 217–37; Michael Allen, "Toward Theological Anthropology: Tracing the Anthropological Principles of John

desires but of a heavenly longing that permeates our living hope and our ethical posture. We now wish to sketch the significance of recovering heavenly-mindedness, in particular, noting the way in which it frames a host of commitments pivotal to Christian faith and practice.

Heaven as Earth's Intellectual Frame

The comparison of Owen's vision of spiritual-mindedness with the earthy and embodied emphases of contemporary theology jars the mind and heart. Contrary to frequently cited suggestions, it is not because Owen or the classical tradition espouses a distant or disembodied hope but because more modern imagination plants our hope in such thin soil. That tension bespeaks not merely a lost topic of theology but a fundamentally different posture through which one explores many things theologically. In this next section, we explore ways in which heavenly-mindedness frames a host of elements of Christian faith and practice.

First, heavenly-mindedness alerts us to the fundamental rest found only in returning unto God himself. Against all forms of instrumentalism, we are warned here that our desire is to be for God, neither simply nor primarily for various benefits provided by this God. We are to be attuned to the startling words of King David: "One thing have I asked of the LORD, that will I seek after: that I may dwell in the house of the LORD all the days of my life, to gaze upon the beauty of the LORD and to inquire in his temple" (Ps 27:4). David, of course, made many requests throughout the

Webster," *International Journal of Systematic Theology* 19, no. 1 (2017): 6–29. A somewhat companionable emphasis upon thinking theologically upon hope and the ethic befitting a living hope necessarily leading to a focus upon heaven can be found in Christopher Morse, *The Difference Heaven Makes: Rehearsing the Gospel as News* (London: T & T Clark, 2010), though the particular exposition of heaven would differ at numerous points.

Psalms; even within this single psalm alone, he asks not only for God to hear him (v. 7) and to forsake him not (v. 9), but also to teach him (v. 11) and to give him "not up to the will of my adversaries" (v. 12). David does bring other things before the Lord. But they are as naught. One thing he has asked. Nothing else is enumerated when it comes time to prioritize. Ultimately, all blessings sought in prayer are reduced or traced back to this fundamental yearning for rest in God, described in terms of dwelling with and seeing God's own face.

Irenaeus of Lyons famously quipped that "the glory of God is man fully alive."[15] Especially since the mid-twentieth century, this phrase has stood front and center to movements in the Roman Catholic world as part of the claims of Henri de Lubac and the *nouvelle théologie*[16] and the wider Protestant mainline world. It has represented an unembarrassed commitment to Christian humanism, suggesting that God does in fact fulfill our deepest aspirations and that the gospel message is not fundamentally misanthropic. This word is crucial. Yet oftentimes the quip comes apart from context, for Irenaeus specified what "man fully alive" meant, pressing on to say "and the life of man consists in beholding God." Christian humanism cannot be pursued apart from the painstaking theological work of redefining the humane end under the prompting of the one true God, whom we have been made to behold.

Second, heavenly-mindedness prompts us to trace the full scope and sequence of Christ's work. In the modern era attention has fixed largely upon the incarnational sojourn of the Word in the first century, whether by way of its affirmation or of deconstruction by cynics. Yet the creedal tradition of the church reminds us that the heralds of the gospel attested a wider work

15. Irenaeus, *Against Heresies* 4.20.7.
16. See especially Henri de Lubac, *Catholicism: Christ and the Common Destiny of Man*, trans. Lancelot Sheppard and Elizabeth Englund (Kent: Burns & Oates Ltd.; repr. San Francisco: Ignatius, 1988).

begun in eternity past ("for us and our salvation he came down from heaven") and furthered into the very presence of God ("he ascended into heaven and is seated at the right hand of God"). The Heidelberg Catechism sought to expound, for example, the angles of the gospel revealed in that exaltation unto heaven:

> Q. 49 What benefit do we receive from Christ's ascension into heaven?
>
> A. First, that he is our Advocate in the presence of his Father in heaven. Second, that we have our flesh in heaven as a sure pledge that he, as the Head, will also take us, his members, up to himself. Third, that he sends us his Spirit as a counterpledge by whose power we seek what is above, where Christ is, sitting at the right hand of God, and not things that are on earth.[17]

Before we think about wider implications of seeking "what is above," we must begin where the text turns appositionally with the phrase "where Christ is" (Col 3:1; cf. Eph 1:20; Col 2:12). Christ is in heaven, and Christ acts as our Advocate in the very presence of our heavenly Father. He is a pledge and, in due time, he "will also take us, his members, up to himself." And the interim period between his advents is not a time of inactivity, for "he sends us his Spirit" to draw our aspirations unto him in heaven itself.

The gospel does not end with the passion, the resurrection, or even the ascension of the incarnate Son. The life-giving work of the Son continues from God's right hand where Jesus Christ reigns and rules over all. That throne room provides the exalted context for the exercise of his prophetic office, so that his word

17. "The Heidelberg Catechism [1563]," in *Reformed Confessions of the Sixteenth Century*, ed. Arthur Cochrane (Louisville: Westminster John Knox, 2003), 313.

is now "living and active" (Heb 4:12–13). Though he has commissioned others to bear his word now, he remains "great shepherd of the sheep" and pastors his flock from on high (Heb 13:20). Whatever the merits of historical Jesus study as it has played out in the last three centuries, we do well to note that the second person of the Son cannot be known first through any such gaze. He must be beheld as one who *is* in heaven and who acts with that heavenly glory.[18]

Third, heavenly-mindedness fixes not only upon God and the exalted Christ but also on the "kingdom of heaven" wherein the divine life makes its salvific mark upon creaturely existence. Contemplation of the heavenly takes in meditative focus on the God who creates, sustains, and brings all things unto their end, for "from him, and through him, and to him are all things" (Rom 11:33). Because of the kind of being God is, we cannot fix our minds and hearts upon him without thereby also pinning them to his kingdom, that is, upon the people and place marked by his lordly work of creation and recreation.

Jonathan Pennington has offered helpful analysis of the Matthean duality of heaven and earth employed so frequently and uniquely in that gospel text (e.g., Matt 3:2; 5:3). In so doing he upends the dominant presumption that Matthew simply substitutes the phrasing "kingdom of heaven" for the more typical "kingdom of God" language out of a pious desire not to name God overtly (owing, so the typical explanation runs, to his Jewish background). Pennington shows that much more is going on with this particular language, and it accents the full range of what is connoted by talk of "heaven" and the "heavenlies" more broadly.

18. Dietrich Ritschl, *Memory and Hope: An Inquiry concerning the Presence of Christ* (New York: Macmillan, 1967). This incisive book is hindered in its historical judgments, however, regarding the Western tradition (eliding the precursors that might be found in Calvin, the Puritans, and the classical Reformed dogmatics of the sixteenth and seventeenth centuries, or even the latter writings of Karl Barth).

"Heaven and earth" for Matthew is not just a figure of speech ("merism" would be the rhetorical term), using a contrasting pair to indicate an all-encompassing whole (as it may be in Genesis 1:1 and similar instances). Rather, the pairing juxtaposes that which is divine and that which is human and sinful, not yet submitting to the divine reign. Pennington even shows how the singular and plural forms of "heaven" signal such distinctions.[19] Tracing the way in which this idiom marks Matthew's argument in various ways—not only from the way he describes the kingdom but also the language of our "heavenly Father" as identifier for God Almighty—Pennington seeks to show that the idiom points toward an eschatological resolution still in flux. Heaven and earth have not yet become coterminous: while God is Lord over heaven now, earth remains very much opposed to his reign.

This trek through Matthean language reminds us that heaven is not merely a cipher for "God" or "the divine" but refers to God's presence with and to the creaturely realm in a lordly manner.[20] Heaven, in other words, takes in the way in which creaturely time, space, and being can be with God. While the language of the "kingdom of heaven" must be defined by the character of the heavenly king who is Father to our Lord Jesus Christ, the "kingdom of heaven" cannot be reduced to the "king of heaven." The kingdom expresses and enjoys the kingly presence, albeit in a creaturely key. Heaven is God's place on earth, though also earth's place with God.

Fourth, heavenly-mindedness provides a reoriented sense of self within the frame of one's heavenly citizenship and enrollment in that eternal kingdom. Paul can speak of a new self, contrasted with both the Jewish heritage of his past (Phil 3:3–8) and the path of pagans around him (3:18–19). He will address those to whom

19. Jonathan T. Pennington, *Heaven and Earth in the Gospel of Matthew* (Leiden: Brill, 2007; repr. Grand Rapids: Baker Academic, 2009), 342.

20. On heaven, see Donald Wood, "Maker of Heaven and Earth," *International Journal of Systematic Theology* 14, no. 4 (2012): esp. 393–95.

he writes as "my brothers" and "my beloved" (4:1), terms that likely refer not to some action he has performed (even the love is not from Paul ultimately) but to God's own naming of them, adopting and bestowing love and favor upon them. Amidst these descriptions he presses on to speak of how "our citizenship is in heaven, and from it we await a savior, the Lord Jesus Christ, who will transform our lowly body to be like his glorious body, by the power that enables him even to subject all things to himself" (3:20–21). Political loyalty takes heavenly form here, with citizenship speaking to a higher identification from which redemption or salvation shall come. That coming descent will transform and subject reality to its own claims, which Paul commends in the most personal form possible ("to himself").

We might think that this is an apocalyptic inversion of a settled sense of self, as if Paul's imagination here has turned the tables on a stable approach to human identity. This language of salvation and transformation coming from on high, in such a scheme, would upend a creational definition of human nature or a substantive depiction of our creaturely character. Yet the end is like the beginning, exceeding it no doubt but in ways that fit its own initial gestures. It is no surprise that citizenship above brings transformation and salvation from without, at least not when we speak of persons who were initially fashioned after the very image of God (Gen 1:26–27).[21] We too often think immediately of faculties and moral characteristics when debating that phraseology in Christian anthropology, connecting the image of God to a part, relation, task, or trait that most closely connects

21. John Calvin's link of creation and consummation, protology and eschatology, has influenced my account heavily; see especially *Institutes of the Christian Religion*, ed. John T. McNeill, trans. Ford Lewis Battles, Library of Christian Classics 20 (Louisville: Westminster John Knox, 2006), II.vi.4; John Calvin, *Commentaries on the First Book of Moses Called Genesis*, vol. 1, trans. John King (Grand Rapids: Eerdmans, 1948), on Gen 2:9; and the helpful analysis of Julie Canlis, *Calvin's Ladder: A Spiritual Theology of Ascent and Ascension* (Grand Rapids: Eerdmans, 2010), 65.

with the Godhead. While the image does speak to our nature, it first commends a difference that connotes our dependence. The difference is this: we are but an image, whereas God is reality. To take up the classical language of Augustine and Peter Lombard, we are but a sign, whereas God is the thing itself.[22] That is the first aspect of image language that can so easily be overlooked: an image is derivative and secondary. Before we talk about any way in which the image bespeaks our similarity to God, we must first note the ever greater dissimilarity conveyed in that very term.

Humanity's secondary or subordinate nature—that we are not self-existent but patterned after another—leads right in to the way in which human nature has always been dependent upon life coming from the outside. Various images attest this, whether a vocal summons to life (Gen 1:26) or a "breath of life" into the dust of the earth (Gen 2:7). Contemporary theologians have attested this characteristic in various ways, speaking of our eccentric existence or of the plasticity of human existence and nature.[23] It is not surprising, then, that faith or the personal appropriation of one's ontological dependence upon God marks the path of human life before God at so many points throughout the biblical plotline. Whether in describing the pathway of Father Abraham or of the struggling Hebrews late in the first century, faith marks the way

22. For classic accounts of the distinction between signs and things, see Augustine, *Teaching Christianity*, ed. John E. Rotelle, trans. Edmund Hill, Works of St. Augustine I/11 (Hyde Park, NY: New City, 1996), 106–7 (I.ii.2); and Peter Lombard, *The Sentences*, vol. 1, *The Mystery of the Trinity*, Mediaeval Sources in Translation 42, trans. Giulio Silano (Toronto: Pontifical Institute of Mediaeval Studies, 2007), 5–11 (dist. 1).

23. David Kelsey, *Eccentric Existence: A Theological Anthropology* (Louisville: Westminster John Knox, 2009); Kathryn Tanner, *Christ the Key*, Current Issues in Theology (Cambridge: Cambridge University Press, 2009), ch. 1. I would express the plasticity of humanity in slightly different ways than does Tanner, distinguishing the change from a transformation of nature per se more than she does and offering a more substantive definition of nature than mere plasticity.

in which the race is to be run because faith alone owns one's call to be an image of one's Maker and Sustainer.

Humans have always lived on borrowed breath and found their identity only above the sun, as was sketched so pointedly by the penetrating criticism of every pathway to self-satisfaction "under the sun" in Ecclesiastes (e.g., Eccl 1:9; 2:11). Thus, in the eschatological contrasts drawn out in Philippians 3, Paul draws our attention ultimately to that highest of heights wherein our eternal identity and ultimate allegiance must finally be located, citizenship in heaven. Heavenly-mindedness extends our anthropological self-analysis by extending our contemplation of our being and nature into the dawning provision of heaven's appearance and the spreading of its glory. Bruce Marshall and Julie Canlis have used the language of an "extrospective" approach to human existence in conveying the Christian notion of the self. We are given being by God and always have our existence as gift. Heavenly-mindedness, in the example of Paul and others (Phil 3:17), reminds us to have a caelospective perspective on the self as well wherein our hearts are lifted up unto God in the heavens.[24]

Humanity cannot be defined simply by any earthly, external forces. Whereas much in contemporary philosophy might veer toward what is often termed individual expressivism,[25] a concurrent trend marks our culture: owing to greater appreciation of the formative strength of social and physical forces at play in

24. Bruce D. Marshall, "Justification as Declaration and Deification," *International Journal of Systematic Theology* 4, no. 1 (2002): 16; Canlis, *Calvin's Ladder*, 146. While finding his language of "extrospection" to be insightful, I have articulated disagreements with Marshall's broader argument in that essay elsewhere (see Allen, *Justification and the Gospel: Understanding the Contexts and Controversies* [Grand Rapids: Baker Academic, 2013], 49–51).

25. Individual expressivism is most powerfully furthered, perhaps, in Michel Foucault, *The Uses of Pleasure*, vol. 2 of *The History of Sexuality*, trans. Robert Hurley (London: Penguin, 1992), 26–28. The idea finds brilliant analysis in Charles Taylor, *Sources of the Self: The Making of Modern Identity* (Cambridge, MA: Harvard University Press, 1989).

our midst and all our stories, the self is simultaneously drawn to a deterministic definition according to material forces before which it is an endless victim. Reinhard Hütter attests the strange mingling of these opposing forces:

> And so, after Kant, Fichte, and Nietzsche on the one hand and Marx, Darwin, and Freud on the other, we find ourselves as late moderns caught on a manic-depressive roller-coaster ride between the ghost of the Promethean daydream of freedom, by now turned desperate and therefore dreaming of autocreativity—that is, of designing our bodies, of choosing our gender, our values, and our destinies freely according to our idiosyncratic likings and longings—and the Hades-like nightmare of endless victimization by "the system"—by anonymous economic, political, and cultural power structures, by our own genetic makeup, and by the will to power of everyone else around us.[26]

John Milbank and Adrian Pabst have recently argued that modern liberal political theory has silently underwritten and furthered a thoroughly materialist view of the self and of society as a gathering of selves.[27] And it is this materialistic impulse, whereby the self is defined in immanent terms (either of one's own styling as in Foucault's pathway or of social formation in its deterministic movements), that is so directly challenged by a heavenly minded sense of self.[28]

---

26. Reinhard Hütter, "(Re-)Forming Freedom: Freedom's Fate in Modernity and Protestantism's Antinomian Captivity," in *Bound to Be Free: Evangelical Catholic Engagements in Ecclesiology, Ethics, and Ecumenism* (Grand Rapids: Eerdmans, 2005), 123.

27. John Milbank and Adrian Pabst, *Politics as Virtue: Post-Liberalism and the Human Future* (London: Rowman & Littlefield, 2016), 379.

28. See especially Craig S. Keener, *The Mind of the Spirit: Paul's Approach to Transformed Thinking* (Grand Rapids: Baker Academic, 2015), 205–51.

A heavenly frame elides both the cynical machinations of social or material determinisms and the glib celebration of self-shaping presumption. The divine descent of the exalted one and his ongoing provision of heavenly gifts (Eph 4:11) call us to identify our very selves not in merely tangible, available, and obvious pathways of sight but by faith in what is ours in the heavenlies (Eph 2:6–7; Col 3:1–5). The same God who walked in the garden of innocence comes victoriously into Zion at the end, in both cases granting life and being to his children. Just as surely as we can look back to the giving of our selves unto us in creation, so we can also look unto the way in which heaven shall return in greater glory at the final advent of our God. In these and no doubt other ways, heavenly-mindedness rules the way in which we imagine the world and our self in light of the Lord of heaven and earth. Far from registering as a mere locus among others, being mindful of heaven flavors and seasons the full range of theological contemplation for it impinges on how we think of God, his incarnation in the person of Jesus, his coming reign, and our very identity and being therein. Though it summons us first unto God and Christ's kingdom, it really does lead to a vital and humane portrait of creaturely dignity.

Heaven as Earth's Lived Form

We have lingered over the way in which heavenly-mindedness truly does summon us to human integrity and goodness by drawing them from the richer soil of God's own life and action. Such, no doubt, runs against suspicions that a celestial bent tilts misanthropic and theomonistic and suffers a net loss regarding sociopolitical activism. Heavenly-mindedness not only shapes the rule of faith whereby we know ourselves and our world in light of the King of Heaven. A life of heavenly-mindedness also marks out the way in which our lives are ordered by providing a form for earthly life as citizens of another kingdom (Phil 3:20). It was the Reformed divine Herman Witsius who said:

> The intent contemplation of the Lord Jesus greatly con-
> tributes. The oftener that a believer beholds him in spirit,
> the more clearly he knows his perfections, of which his
> holiness is the ornament. The more clearly he knows
> them, the more ardently he loves them. The more ar-
> dently he loves them, the more like to them he desires to
> become. For love aspires after a likeness to the beloved;
> nay, in love itself there is already a great similitude: for,
> "God is love," 1 John iv.8. Moreover, the more ardently
> he loves God, he will both the more frequently, the more
> willingly and attentively behold him; and thus often run-
> ning round that circle of beholding and loving, for ever
> returning into itself, he gains by every act a new feature
> of this most glorious image.[29]

Contemplation of the heavenly beauty of the Christ leads to love of and conformity unto that same incarnate Son who is himself truth and goodness. A number of studies, ranging from the philosophical to the exegetical, have traced out the way in which we become what we love.[30] We seek more and more conformity to what we love—and we are elicited more intently by what we love. Heavenly-mindedness thus shapes our moral ends and also motivates us with celestial encouragements.

29. Herman Witsius, *The Economy of the Covenants between God and Man* (Phillipsburg, NJ: Presbyterian & Reformed, 1990), 2:42.

30. See especially James K. A. Smith, *You Are What You Love: The Spiritual Power of Habit* (Grand Rapids: Brazos, 2016); and especially the more detailed philosophical account found in his *Imagining the Kingdom: How Worship Works* (Grand Rapids: Baker Academic, 2013); for an exegetical tracing of these themes through the whole canon, see G. K. Beale, *We Become What We Worship: A Biblical Theology of Idolatry* (Downers Grove, IL: IVP Academic, 2008).

First, heavenly-mindedness forms our desire by helping to order our loves. We begin again with the psalmist's prayer: "One thing have I asked of the LORD, that will I seek after: that I may dwell in the house of the LORD all the days of my life, to gaze upon the beauty of the LORD and to inquire in his temple" (Ps. 27:4). The reader of this psalm can be forgiven for thinking, at first glance, that David is self-forgetful in the wrong sort of way. Indeed, before this very psalm ends, he will ask for deliverance from his adversaries who lay false charges at his feet (27:12). The whole Psalter regularly witnesses to his concern for relational, political, and military matters, taking requests of all sorts before the Lord. Yet here stands this witness that he asks but "one thing," namely, that he be with God. Imagery of the household and of the temple evokes the nearness and the favor involved in that wish; mention of gaze upon the beauty of God and inquiring of him speak to the intimacy latent in this emphasis. This prioritized request bespeaks a desire, a longing, and affection. His love is ordered.

Jeremiah Burroughs saw a similar focus or ordering revealed in the final words of the psalmist. 2 Samuel 23:5 commends God's salvation and covenant even in the face of the onslaught of his political opposition.[31] Earthly threats may loom, yet heavenly peace is to be sought always. And the later Davidic king will teach his own to pray for many things (Matt 6:8–13). Though he comes as the bread of heaven and cup of salvation, he does not consider a request for "daily bread" to be beneath his followers (Matt 6:11). Yet, like David, he does speak of the one thing and of ordering loves in this sermon: "Seek first the kingdom of God and his righteousness, and all these thing will be added to you" (6:33). The heavenly is not nearer God, Barth says, but God nearer the heavenly, and that makes all the difference.[32] He was attesting

31. Jeremiah Burroughs, *The Rare Jewel of Christian Contentment* (Edinburgh: Banner of Truth Trust, 1964), 78–81.
32. Karl Barth, *The Doctrine of Creation*, vol. 3 of *Church Dogmatics*, ed.

something deep in the catholic and Reformed tradition, as put beautifully by Alexander Whyte:

> The Scriptures constantly teach that man's only true happiness is in God, and that his full happiness in God cannot be attained in this life, but that believing men have that happiness assured to them in the life to come. Commenting on John 14:6, Godet says, "Jesus here substitutes the Father for the Father's house. For it is not in heaven that we are to find God, but in God that we are to find heaven."[33]

Heavenly-mindedness forms in us the right sort of priorities, wherein God is all in all (1 Cor 15:28).

Such a theological focus is counter-intuitive and counter-cultural this side of Eden, even amidst very religious sects. "The mind becomes insensitive to heavenly desire through its preoccupation with early cares. When its preoccupation with the actions of the world hardens it, it cannot be softened for the things that pertain to God's love."[34] Hardening of this sort comes naturally to the self-infatuated sinner and is propelled by the materialistic frame of modern culture. Paul attests that "we all once lived in the passions of our flesh, carrying out the desires of the body and the mind" (Eph 2:3). In context, this flows forth from what is true "by nature" as well as what pressure comes from the demonic and social spheres. But God calls us to lift up our hearts to look upon the "heavenly places in Christ Jesus" where we are filled with "the fullness of him who fills all in all," that is, "with all the fullness

---

G. W. Bromiley and T. F. Torrance, trans. G. W. Bromiley and R. J. Ehrlich (Edinburgh: T & T Clark, 1960), 3:422–23.

33. Alexander Whyte, *An Exposition on the Shorter Catechism* (Grand Rapids: Christian Heritage, 2004), 137.

34. Gregory the Great, "Homily 19," in *Forty Gospel Homilies*, trans. Dom David Hurst (Kalamazoo, MI: Cistercian, 1990), 145 (on Luke 10:1–7).

of God" (Eph 1:23; 3:19). Heavenly-mindedness molds our desires for something eternal and infinite, for God's own fullness and nothing less. While we may receive much else besides, heavenly-mindedness forms us to ask for this "one thing."

Second, heavenly-mindedness norms the posture or manner with which we participate in religious protocols and practices. Sarah Coakley has noted the way in which religious exercises can be commodified. She observes that recent focus upon practices (over against mere ideals or personal experiences) must be molded in a particular way lest we manipulate them: "In short, the undertaking of ascetic 'practice' is not one that comes with instant, commodifiable effects. Fashionable as the notion of 'practice' has become in recent philosophy and anthropology . . . , it is, alas, no less subject to ethical trivialization than those more abstract philosophical trends to which it was intended as a corrective."[35] Practices do not deliver immediate, manageable results of a material, empirical sort.

Jesus himself warns against objectifying approaches to religious rites. He will berate the hypocrites who pray to be heard by others, suggesting "they have their reward" and presumably will receive no more from God (Matt 6:5). He also lambasts those who would seek to overwhelm God with words, "heap[ing] up empty phrases as the Gentiles do, for they think that they will be heard for their many words" (6:7). Religious protocols, such as prayer, do not serve to manipulate God, nor do they serve primarily to deliver earthly benefits. "Your Father knows what you need before you ask him" (6:8). Prayer serves to bind us together with God so that the provision of our needs (even the flippant needs that we share with the lilies of the field and the birds of the air: so 6:26, 28) occurs in a way that draws us into this covenantal communion (precisely what the lilies and the birds lack).

35. Sarah Coakley, *The New Asceticism: Sexuality, Gender, and the Quest for God* (London: Bloomsbury, 2015), 101–2.

What, then, of earthly realities, blessings and needs in this life for material matters? The Bible often employs earthly benefits as signs of God's favor. Augustine frequently noted how often members of "the synagogue" would misperceive the "symbolic" character of these gifts and believe that they were the final goal. The famed bishop of Hippo thought that only a few had the spiritual perception to see through these goods the transposed glory promised in God himself.[36] One of the most poignant concerns of Dutch neo-Calvinism has been the way in which Herman Bavinck and others have sought to affirm the non-spiritualized eschatology of the Bible.[37] Most recently, Richard Middleton has sought to show that these Old Testament blessings ought to provide a necessary context, hermeneutically speaking, for reading later New Testament statements regarding the blessings of God sought through our covenant with him.[38] In so doing, Middleton has caught a key emphasis of Reformed hermeneutics and, indeed, of covenant theology, namely, that we read the Bible sequentially and allow the Old to frame our approach to the New. He has gone well beyond even Bavinck by rereading spiritual language in the New Testament in the earthy tones supposedly drawn by the Old Testament.

John Calvin believed that such a reading of the Old was massively problematic (as it was prefigured, we might say, in the charges of the Anabaptists of his own day). Calvin argued, tracing out Augustinian logic, that while many individual Israelites focused overly much upon earthly goods as the result of religious devotion to Israel's God, the faithful always caught what the

36. See, e.g., Augustine, *Expositions of the Psalms [51–72]*, Works of St. Augustine III/17, ed. John Rotelle, trans. Maria Boulding (Hyde Park, NY: New City, 2001), 475–76 (on Psalm 72).

37. See, e.g., Bavinck, *Reformed Dogmatics*, ed. John Bolt, trans. John Vriend (Grand Rapids: Baker Academic, 2008), 4:720.

38. See esp. J. Richard Middleton, *A New Heaven and a New Earth: Reclaiming Biblical Eschatology* (Grand Rapids: Baker Academic, 2014), 78, 95, 97, 105–7.

Scriptures plainly revealed: God transmitted his greatest glory—his own fullness shared with us—through these lesser parables of the good.[39] The earthly kingdom is a crowning blessing, but the heavenly throne is the gem at its very crest.

The covenant teaches that religious devotion—typified by keeping religious practices and rites (e.g., Sabbath)—does trigger life that goes well in the land (e.g., Exod 20:12; Deut 6:1; 12:1; 26:1; 27:2). The maker of all things is not ambivalent regarding their flourishing. But Israel then and followers of Jesus now can and should and do learn that the land is not the ultimate goal, for their maker has fashioned them in such a way that lesser goods cannot provide what is ultimately significant and apart from the greater gift of ultimate significance will not even continue to be received as gifts. Indeed, the land is a blessing because God is there, and only as such. The pursuit of the land through devotion pleases God because it involves our dependent engagement of God in distinctly personal ways. Moses knew that other, lesser gifts cannot be satisfying apart from God's pledged presence (Exod 33:15–16).[40] Religion can never be depersonalized so long as its heavenly bent is always kept front and center, for heaven comes in intrinsically personal fashion or not at all.

Third, heavenly-mindedness shapes the manner of our confessing sin and expressing lament before God. We can begin here by considering how heavenly-mindedness frames our anguished confession of our sin. Again the psalmist jars our attention, for his contrite words in Psalm 51 bespeak the remorse and anguish of one

39. See esp. Calvin, *Institutes of the Christian Religion*, 1:428–57 (II.x–II.xi.8).

40. It is instructive that the Exodus was not primarily about liberation but fundamentally about the demonstration of God's supremacy over Pharaoh and Egypt, according to Jon D. Levenson, "Exodus and Liberation," in *The Hebrew Bible, the Old Testament, and Historical Criticism: Jews and Christians in Biblical Studies* (Louisville: Westminster John Knox, 1993), 127–59 (where he notes that this priority shapes the definitively spiritual facet of even liberation in the Exodus, 147).

who has been jolted into a grim self-awareness of his terrible guilt (cf. 2 Sam 12:1–15). "Against you, you only, have I sinned and done what is evil in your sight" (Ps 51:5). The reader attuned to the wider story might hesitate here, wondering what of Bathsheba he raped (2 Sam. 11:3–4), of Uriah he murdered (2 Sam 11:14–17), and of Israel whom he manipulated for his own ends throughout. Surely God has been sinned against; indeed, we read that "the thing that David had done displeased the LORD" (2 Sam 11:27). But can we really follow his confession and its claim that "Against you, you only, have I sinned"?

David's words prompt us to consider the gravity of sin precisely as they summon us to the central facet of sin.[41] We rightly note the social consequences of sin in its manifold forms. Sin impinges upon and affects others, oftentimes in ripple effects that go well beyond the intended parties immediate to the situation. Responsibility for citizens and neighbors, children and parents, siblings and lovers, plays out in interwoven ways. Indeed, we can go still further and note the ecological or environmental impact of sin, as attested in Genesis 3:17 and Romans 8:22. The breadth of sin's impact and of its ongoing influence was registered by Paul himself. Writing to the Ephesians, he spoke of their plight: "And you were dead in the trespasses and sins in which you once walked, following the course of this world, following the prince of the power of the air, the spirit that is now at work in the sons of disobedience—among whom we all once lived in the passions of our flesh, carrying out the desires of the body and the mind, and were by nature children of wrath, like the rest of mankind" (Eph 2:1–3). Sin impacts the spiritual relations ("the prince of the power of the air"), social contexts ("the course of this world"), the misdirected desires ("the passions of our flesh"), and the self's nature ("by nature children of wrath").

41. For a helpful survey of the multi-pronged portrayal of sin here, see Christopher B. Ansberry, "Writings," in *T & T Clark Companion to the Doctrine of Sin*, ed. Keith L. Johnson and David Lauber (London: T & T Clark, 2016), 46–53.

Does the Bible's instruction regarding our problem only take the form of alerting us to its breadth, what some might call the totality of our depravity? While the Scriptures do alert us to the extensive circumference, they also point anew to the character of the very center of our ills. Meditation upon heaven itself reorients us to that most aggrieved party in our every transgression. Admittedly, God does not have lobbyists, and our misdeeds against him are not inveighed against as might be the corporate misdeeds, familial grievances, or governmental abuse reported in the daily news. But the heavenly minded person remembers that always in the very middle of any situation of struggle is our sin against the triune God. While the ripple effects of our sin do reach out to countless others, we nonetheless need to remember always to deal first and foremost with our plight as sinners before the holy God. John Calvin offered a compelling sketch of this prioritization, as capably summarized by Heiko Oberman: "Calvin is intent to follow the biblical story and vocabulary by portraying created man as 'in communion with God' and fallen man as 'alienated from God.' . . . When the *imago Dei* is lost, then this is not a loss in 'substance' or 'essence,' but in orientation."[42]

As observed earlier, though, heavenly-mindedness also molds the way that we experience and lament loss of varied sorts. We are prompted by countless others to note ways in which we struggle. The market analyst or broker reports the daily register of dropping stock prices. The M.D. sits one down to give an update on the wellness (or lack thereof) of one's body after the battery of labs, tests, and physical exams. We are trained in these and other spheres to observe struggles and frustrations. The Bible presses further, however, to teach us to truly lament loss by taking it be-

42. Heiko Oberman, "The Pursuit of Happiness: Calvin between Humanism and Reformation," in *Humanity and Divinity in Renaissance and Reformation*, ed. John O'Malley (New York: Brill, 1993), 265–66 (cited in Canlis, *Calvin's Ladder*, 85).

fore God. Doing so involves not only owning up to God himself about our loss of other things, though this is a significant facet of Christian lament, but more importantly it involves the summons to name our sorrow over lost or lacking spiritual communion and celestial blessedness owing to some distance from God's favor. Again we see the psalmist schooling us in taking the struggles of the day—even the tangible threat of the enemy (Ps 13:2, 4)—before God, albeit by tying it to its more ultimate issue: "How long will you hide your face from me?" (13:1).

Sorrow and lament express faith and delight in God.[43] Frustration comes naturally, but a genuine sense of anguish over loss requires the experience of God's good gifts and a growing awareness of our need for them. Such sorrow must match the degree of the good, however, or else we make mountains out of molehills and miss the truly grievous instances of misery. In this way we can see how Jesus was styled the "man of sorrows" in as much as he uniquely knew the severity of moving from that most intimate fellowship with the Father toward the ignominious God-forsakeness of the cross, when he cried out the psalmist's words: "My God, my God, why have you forsaken me?" (Mark 15:34; see also Ps 22:1).[44] Precisely owing to his remarkable level of beloved communion with his Father and because he had always perfectly known the divine pleasure, he was able to mark its absence in a more excruciating register than any other lament. As we look to that divine smile that is and will be ours in Christ, we too can learn to lament and confess with greater verve and in an appropriately deeper blues tone.

43. On lament as a practice of faith, see J. Todd Billings, *Rejoicing in Lament: Wrestling with Incurable Cancer and Life in Christ* (Grand Rapids: Brazos, 2015), esp. 35–54.

44. See Kelly Kapic, "Psalm 22: Forsakenness and the God Who Sings," in *Theological Commentary: Evangelical Essays*, ed. Michael Allen (London: T & T Clark, 2011), 41–56; see the argument elaborated further in Kelly Kapic, *Embodied Hope: A Theological Meditation on Pain and Suffering* (Downers Grove, IL: IVP Academic, 2017).

Fourth, heavenly-mindedness directs the extent and way with which we pursue and receive earthly goods of all sorts. The Bible does not draw one away from acknowledgment of creaturely goods. The repeated approval of God himself recurs throughout the first creation account (Gen 1:3, 10, 12, 18, 21, 25), signaling what will be explicitly stated in the following chapter: "You may surely eat of every tree of the garden" other than "the tree of the knowledge of good and evil" (Gen 2:16). God names created reality—the sun and moon above and the fruits of the earth—as created goods in the beginning and summons humans to partake.

Such invitation to enjoy the created goods of God is not merely an aspect of our beginning but also of our intended end, for we confess: "I believe in the resurrection of the body." And we find that our own anticipated resurrection matches the created and embodied goodness of that which marked our incarnate and glorified Savior (1 Cor 15:48–49). Jesus communicates or makes common those blessings he receives from his heavenly Father to those who are united to him by faith—that is the gospel message (so, e.g., Luke 24:47; Acts 5:31). The Bible points to many such blessings, with communion with God being the highest and most fundamental. The creed reminds us, however, that there are other crucial facets to the many-splendored beneficence of Christ's work. The same glorified body enjoyed now by our incarnate and risen Lord shall be ours, for he is the firstfruits of that resurrection (e.g., Rom 6:5; 1 Cor 15:49).

In prompting our attention to the bodily benefit of Christ's redemptive work, the creed signals a wider reality: the universality or totality of the reconciling and restorative work of Jesus Christ. While the Bible does not present a universalism by which all persons are reunited with their God (against which see the words of Jesus in John 5:29 and elsewhere), the Bible does portray a universalism whereby all things are reconciled unto God and every facet of the redeemed is restored and renewed in him (see esp. Col 1:15–20 with its repetition of the language of "all").

In other words, the people of God are not saved by being siphoned through a strainer with only some ultimate or most spiritual portion being kept as an apportioned remainder, whether that might be an intellect or a soul. Quite the contrary, the biblical portrait involves the remarkable claim that Christ Jesus has come to reconcile all things and to renew every facet of human existence. Those redeemed are, in fact, restored in whole, for the Savior says: "Behold, I am making all things new" (Rev 21:5).

How might we think about this new earthiness and embodiment? Here we must suggest that intellectual humility is in order, and we can first see this need from the way that the risen and glorified body is described. Humility is demanded of us, for the portrayals of bodily glory involve not only mundane or common realities but also incomprehensible or strange incandescence. The glorified Jesus does bear his earlier wounds (such that he can invite Thomas to touch them; so John 20:27; Luke 24:38–40), and he does even partake of the fish of the sea (Luke 24:41–43). Yet the glorified Christ suddenly appears in rooms, seemingly without walking through any doorway; his disappearing acts (as evident earlier in John 20:19 and Luke 24:36–37) are equally quick and mysterious. And while his wounds are recognizable, two of his disciples do not identify him during a lengthy stroll, finally catching a sense of his identity when he breaks bread with them (Luke 24:13–31). This mixture of bodily realism and yet glorious mystery was prefigured, to some extent, in the account of the transfiguration (Matt 17:1–8). There Jesus was identifiable in bodily form, differentiated, for example, from Moses and Elijah. And yet the way in which he and his clothes radiated the light of God surely exceeded the bounds of verbal expression to the extent that viewers wound up on their knees and in need of the word: "Fear not" (Matt 17:7). This pairing of the mundane and ordinary with the strange and glorious must prompt reticence to speculate too far and humility to admit that eschatological bodily glory exceeds our explanatory grasp now.

We must go a step further, though, and see that grace does not merely involve the restoration of the natural, as if newness involves mere refurbishment. We rightly hymn the grace that is greater than all our sin, but we do well to remember that glory is greater still than the undoing of sin's deleterious consequences. Grace brings one unto glory, which is itself an escalation beyond the innocence of Eden. To think well about earthly good, we must not only appreciate its metaphysical integrity but also its spiritual relativity before the escalated goodness to which the Creator summons us.

Paul commends this escalation in his writing to the Corinthians. "There are heavenly bodies and earthly bodies, but the glory of the heavenly is of one kind, and the glory of the earthly is of another" (1 Cor 15:40). Paul begins here with a principle regarding all creaturely reality, which he will quickly liken unto the varying degrees of celestial illumination that are plain to the eye, "for star differs from star in glory" (15:41). But he then hones in his focus upon eschatological glory: "So it is with the resurrection of the dead" (15:42). A series of contrasts draw out the still-greater glory of that which is raised compared to that which is sown. What is sown is perishable; what is raised is imperishable. It is sown in dishonor; it is raised in glory. It is sown in weakness; it is raised in power. It is sown a natural body; it is raised a spiritual body. If there is a natural body, there is also a spiritual body (15:43–44). The contrasts vary in their clarity, and a case could surely be made that at least some of them seem to juxtapose the fallen state with the redeemed state (e.g., especially "dishonor" over against "glory"). Yet the final pairing, to which the language seems to be escalating, couples "natural" and "spiritual" rather than "sinful" or "fleshly" (in a Pauline sense) over against "spiritual" or "holy." Paul seems to be suggesting that the eschatological glory exceeds even the protological purity of Edenic existence.

Glory outbids even innocence. Paul's shift to argument by citation seems to confirm this move: "Thus it is written, 'The first man Adam became a living being'" (15:45). He unpacks the movement from that "first" experience of life to attest still further graces: "the last Adam became a life-giving Spirit. But it is not the spiritual that is first but the natural, and then the spiritual. The first man was from the earth, a man of dust; the second man is from heaven" (15:45–47). Richard Gaffin has shown how this intratextual argument shows that the heavenly outbids the earthly, in as much as the "spiritual" surpasses the "natural."[45]

What does it mean for the heavenly to exceed the earthly? Perhaps no area of biblical concern so demonstrates this relationship as that of marriage. Remember that Jesus tells us that one of the key pillars of society today will be absent from that great bliss, for humans will no longer give themselves man to woman as husband and wife (Matt 22:29–30). Interpreting this biting statement (part of his polemic against the Sadducees [Matt 22:23–33]) canonically, we see that marriage does not end in eternity. Rather, marriage is perfected, in as much as the great marriage of the Lamb and his Bride is celebrated there (Rev 21:9). The fellowship and oneness symbolized so powerfully in the earthly marriage of a man and a woman (Eph 5:25–33, esp. v. 32) need no longer occur because its typological fulfillment has been fully and finally brought to pass through the definitive identification, union, communion, and covenant fellowship of Christ and his church.

The perfection of marriage serves as an intellectual prompt for thinking about the social facets of our eschatological hope more broadly. On the one hand, we see the deepest purpose of marriage perfected by human communion being transposed into the ultimate divine-human covenantal fellowship and intimate presence. Thus, our current commitment to marriage has integ-

45. Richard B. Gaffin Jr., *Resurrection and Redemption: A Study in Paul's Soteriology*, 2nd ed. (Phillipsburg, NJ: Presbyterian & Reformed, 1987), 78–91; see also Benjamin Gladd, "The Last Adam as the 'Life-Giving Spirit' Revisited: A Possible OT Background of One of Paul's Most Perplexing Phrases," *Westminster Theological Journal* 71 (2009): 297–309.

rity and deserves our concern and commitment, precisely because it prepares for and is perfected in eternity to come. On the other hand, marriage will no longer exist in its current social form. It will no longer be marked by sexual activity, by procreation as a related end, and so forth. If marriage's perfection involves such radical changes to its reality, we must be humble in our expectations about what other social realities might be like in that new creational hereafter.

In light of these examples—the bodily nature of human glory (as seen in Jesus) or the social nature of human glory (as foretold with regard to marriage by Jesus)—we do well to keep our eye on broader theological principles. Our concern to keep first things first need not and should not undermine our simultaneous commitment to be alert to other facets of canonical teaching.[46] Emphases and priorities cannot foreclose awareness of the breadth of scriptural teaching. In this case, understanding the center of our hope as communion with God in Christ (so powerfully typified by that doctrine of the beatific vision) ought not lead to dismissing or denigrating the earthy aspect of our hope as one involving a bodily resurrection and a new creation in its holistic totality. That said, the fact that other aspects of this broad eschatological vision are not at the center but on its edges should prompt a greater appreciation for the epistemological limits of our understanding of their nature. Without undermining the integrity of bodies, of societies, of place, and of other non-human creatures, we must remember that there are limits to our grasp of their final form. Eschatology, like other doctrines but in a particularly poignant way, must be pursued by faith and by faith alone.

46. Here we can note that Donald Gowan's emphasis on the breadth of the eschatological hope of Israel fails to note its center in communion with God; the new creational breadth ought not be narrowed or thinned, though it must encircle the focal point of God's indwelling and never exist apart from that theocentric core (cf. *Eschatology in the Old Testament*).

Hope will shape behavior. This eschatological and escalated sense of the greater glory of marriage with God in Christ helps reframe our experience of marriage in this life or of the path of celibacy. Sarah Coakley points to a united concern in these two vocations, noting that "the godly ordering of desire is what *conjoins* the ascetic aims of marriage and celibacy, at their best, and equally what judges both of them, at their worst."[47] If such a "conjoining" seems odd or even forced at first, we can see her elaboration of the connection, as she shows that "the reflective, faithful celibate and the reflective, faithful married person may have more in common—by way of prayerful surrendering of inevitably thwarted desire to God—than the unreflective or faithless celibate, or the carelessly happy, or indeed unhappily careless, married person."[48] Marital bliss is a created good (Gen 2:18–25), though even its "reflective, faithful" embrace proves to be less than the greater glory of celestial communion with the God revealed in Christ.

Too often, anxiety concerning the decline of sexual fidelity has led to a focus on the family when, biblically, the focus surely points toward the fact that, married or not, one's body belongs to the Lord (1 Cor 6:13). The degree to which heavenly-mindedness has been excised from Protestant theological imagination can be measured by the temerity with which we read the words of Paul regarding the higher calling of celibacy in 1 Corinthians 7:1–16.[49] Heavenly-mindedness helps alert us to the underlying eschatology that prompted Paul to speak of the greater goodness of purposive celibacy in this life, what Coakley had referred to as "reflective, faithful celibacy." As she ruminates on Gregory of Nyssa's *On Virginity*, Coakley observes the specific issue: "Gregory lauds

47. Coakley, *The New Asceticism*, 30 (emphasis original).
48. Coakley, *The New Asceticism*, 39.
49. I have been most helped in reading 1 Corinthians 5–7 by Alistair May, *The Body for the Lord: Sex and Identity in 1 Corinthians 5–7*, Library of New Testament Studies (London: T & T Clark, 2004).

'virginity' *not* on account of its sexlessness, but because of its with-drawal from *worldly* interests—the building up of families, status and honour—and hence its emulation of the changeless life of the Trinity. It is not sex that is the problem, but worldly values."[50]

Our intended ascent unto heaven itself now prompts a willing contentment in plenty and in want (Phil 4:11; 2 Cor 9:8). Indeed, it prompts a reordering of loves such that lesser goods are loved less than greater goods and, invariably, sacrificed for the sake of those greater goods. Christian asceticism flows from an eschatological framing of life between heaven and earth rather than some meta-physical animus regarding the bodily or creaturely. John Calvin suggested that the motivation unto self-denial and any ascetic discipline must always be by means of greater eschatological de-sire, for "the only way to make right progress in the Gospel is to be attracted by the sweet fragrance of Christ so that we desire Him enough to bid the enticements of the world farewell."[51]

Does this mean abdication of earthly concern? No, relativiza-tion does not equal total renunciation.[52] The same Origen of Al-

---

50. Coakley, *The New Asceticism*, 50 (emphases original), reflecting upon Gregory of Nyssa, "On Virginity," in *Ascetical Works*, trans. Virginia Woods Callahan, Fathers of the Church 58 (Washington, DC: Catholic University of America Press, 1967), 3–75. Admittedly, Coakley's reading of Nyssa more broadly regarding gender can be tendentious at points; for a more his-torically helpful analysis of this text in particular, see also Hans Boersma, *Embodiment and Virtue in Gregory of Nyssa: An Anagogical Approach*, Oxford Early Christian Studies (New York: Oxford University Press, 2012), 117–27. That broader historiographic disagreement does not mar or minimize the significance of the specific point drawn out here by Coakley.

51. See John Calvin, *The Second Epistle of Paul to the Corinthians and the Epistles to Timothy, Titus, and Philemon*, ed. David W. Torrance and Thomas F. Torrance, trans. T. A. Smail, Calvin's New Testament Commentaries (Grand Rapids: Eerdmans, 1964), 34 (on 2 Cor. 2:14). Unfortunately Canlis's account of ascent and ascension in Calvin employs the term "asceticism" only in pe-jorative fashion (*Calvin's Ladder*, 247, 249).

52. For a more subtle assessment of the kind of renunciation advocated by Calvin, in step not only with the Reformational doctrine of grace found in Luther but also (much more widely) with the approach to discipleship rooted

exandria who said, "Anyone, moreover, who asks after mundane and minor matters from God is disregarding the one who commands us to request what is heavenly and great from the God who does not know how to bestow anything mundane or minor," also said: "We should pray then, praying for principal gifts, for those that are truly great and heavenly, and the matter of the shadows that accompany these principal gifts should be left to God, who knows what we need for our perishable body 'before we ask him' (Matt 6.8)."[53] Leaving such matters to God does not mean going voiceless, though, as both the psalmist and the Lord's Prayer attest ("give us this day"). The same God who provides the bread of heaven and the cup of salvation does summon us to ask for daily bread. But he does pledge us difficulty and calls us to faithfully find contentment in him alone.

In at least these four ways, then, heavenly-mindedness shapes our lived experience here in this earthly season wherein we journey through the "kingdom of earth" *en route* to the globalized and ultimate attainment of the "kingdom of heaven." A particular focus upon God, self, and world in this heavenly register and with what we might call eschatological intensity prompts a range of inflections upon the way in which we love and receive love.

Ordering Loves with Augustine

Why does heavenly-mindedness have such widespread entailments? To understand the significance and scope of this focus, we must consider its relationship to the Christian call to love, which is central to the life evoked by the gospel. Augustine serves as a

---

in earlier catholic sources, see David Fink, "Un-Reading Renunciation: Luther, Calvin, and the 'Rich Young Ruler,'" *Modern Theology* 32, no. 4 (2016): 569–93.

53. Origen, "On Prayer," in *Tertullian, Cyprian, and Origen, On the Lord's Prayer*, trans. Alistair Stewart-Sykes (Crestwood, NY: St. Vladimir's Seminary Press, 2004), 16.1 (p. 149) and 17.2 (p. 152).

helpful prompt to explore this link. The rule of faith and rule of love shape Christian reading of Holy Scripture and have done so since the time of the famed bishop of Hippo. Augustine offered a host of principles for how we receive the instruction of the prophets and apostles to our profit, chief among them the constant canon of whether or not a given instance of Christian instruction furthers these two rules.[54] In so doing, he sought to help us read the Bible for God and, conversely, to read the Bible without lapsing into idolatry.

Heavenly-mindedness serves as a constant program of "protocols against idolatry."[55] Such protocols exist for good reason. The sixteenth-century reformer John Calvin famously referred to our hearts as idol-making factories.[56] In recent years Old Testament theologian Walter Brueggemann has noted that "the issue for God's people is characteristically wrong God and not no God."[57] Such ill-fated turns seem to arise time and again, in testaments old and new, and so it is not surprising to see that the apostles must address idolatry head-on, much like the prophets of old. Moshe Halbertal and Avishai Margalit argue, "The central theological principle of the Bible [is] the rejection of idolatry."[58] The Bible begins by relativizing the great lights as entities summoned into being by the only true God (Gen 1:1–2:4) and then ends by reminding us that even the angelic host cannot receive the worship

54. Augustine, *On Christian Teaching*, trans. R. P. H. Green (Oxford: Oxford University Press, 1997), 27 (I.86–88).

55. Nicholas Lash, *The Beginning and End of "Religion"* (Cambridge: Cambridge University Press, 1996), 194.

56. Calvin, *Institutes of the Christian Religion*, 108 (I.xi.8). Calvin made similar comments in his exegetical material: e.g., John Calvin, *Commentaries on the Prophet Ezekiel*, vol. 1, trans. Thomas Myers, Calvin's Commentaries (Grand Rapids: Eerdmans, 1948), 80 (on Ezek. 1:13); Calvin, *The Second Epistle of Paul to the Corinthians*, 141 (on 2 Cor. 11:3).

57. Walter Brueggemann, "Foreword," *Journal of Preachers* 26 (Easter 2003): 1.

58. Moshe Halbertal and Avishai Margalit, *Idolatry*, trans. Naomi Goldblum (Cambridge, MA: Harvard University Press, 1992), 10.

due only to that Lord (Rev 21:8–9). God's Word calls us away from false objects of love and worship and back unto the heavenly king.

Beginning to end, not only in the Scripture but in each of our lives, we need to remember who is of gravest consequence. It may prove helpful to turn now to some doctrinal resources that have been employed in the tradition to ward off idolatry. We have addressed the dangers of tendencies in modern Reformed theology that we have termed eschatological naturalism, a bent toward the elevation of the earthy, embodied, and material as that of ultimate significance. Perhaps it is fitting, then, to return to Augustine himself, lingering over the ways in which he warned against any such overinflation of creaturely significance and summoned us unto singular devotion to the one true God.

First, Augustine spoke of use (*uti*) and enjoyment (*frui*) in *On Christian Teaching*. He argued that God alone was to be enjoyed and other beings or things were to be used. "Enjoyment, after all, consists in clinging to something lovingly for its own sake, while use consists in referring what has come your way to what your love aims at obtaining, provided, that is, that it deserves to be loved."[59] He was not advocating objectifying or commodifying persons, as if our fellow human beings were but mere instruments relationally. But he did suggest that all other creaturely realities are instruments of a sort, in as much as they are metaphysically derivative and thus never relationally or morally ultimate.[60] In other words, the distinction was meant to ward off idolatry in our efforts to relate to one another. Eventually, though, he did find his language to be inelegant and less than helpful, as it deployed

59. Augustine, *Teaching Christianity*, Works of St. Augustine I/11, ed. John E. Rotelle, trans. Mario Naldini et al. (Hyde Park, NY: New City, 1996), 107–8 (I.4.4); cf. 22.20–21.

60. He refers even to the triune persons as "the things therefore that are to be enjoyed," suggesting an ease with objectifying or less than obviously personal language throughout the discussion and not merely with regard to the human or creaturely element to be "used" (108 [I.5.5]).

a rather crass term ("use") that does not straightforwardly or obviously convey the calling of love or even of personal interaction.

Second, when Augustine realized the potentially misleading nature of the distinction as formulated in that text, he modified the distinction in less misleading forms to speak instead of love "for itself" over against love "for God."[61] This later move managed to speak always and everywhere of personal and loving relations, both upward to God and outward to neighbors and even enemies on the human plane. But it continued to differentiate between the ultimate and penultimate in an effort to help prompt single-minded worship of God. Reflecting on the words of Psalm 73:25—"Whom have I in heaven but you? And there is nothing on earth that I desire besides you"—Augustine said: *"He is the God of my heart, and God is my portion for eternity. His heart has become chaste, for now God is loved disinterestedly: the psalmist asks no other reward from God except God."*[62]

Perhaps no lesson gleaned from Augustine matches the abiding significance of ordering our loves.[63] Indeed, one might trace

61. See Augustine, *De catechizandis rudibus.* 7.11.

62. Augustine, "Exposition of Psalm 72," in *Expositions of the Psalms, 51–72*, Works of Saint Augustine III/17, ed. John E. Rotelle, trans. Maria Boulding (Hyde Park, NY: New City, 2001), 491 (XXXII). For a parallel judgment exegetically regarding the significance of the sight of God, see Grant D. Bayliss, *The Vision of Didymus the Blind: A Fourth-Century Virtue Origenism* (New York: Oxford University Press, 2016), 155n80 (on Didymus the Blind, *Commentary on Zechariah*, 2.219.10–15 [3.137]).

63. Incisive accounts of Augustine's ordering of loves may be found in Oliver O'Donovan, *The Problem of Self-Love in St. Augustine* (New Haven: Yale University Press, 1980; repr. Eugene, OR: Wipf & Stock, 2006); Charles Mathewes, *A Theology of Public Life*, Cambridge Studies in Christian Doctrine (Cambridge: Cambridge University Press, 2007), where he helpfully contrasts the eschatological vision of Augustine with more recent claims to developing a purportedly apocalyptic imagination; Charles Mathewes, *The Republic of Grace: Augustinian Thoughts for Dark Times* (Grand Rapids: Eerdmans, 2010), esp. 220–36. Much further work remains to be done extending the work of O'Donovan and Mathewes on the way in which Augustinian ordering of loves functions across the various loci of Christian theology.

all other theological principles in one way or another back to this fundamental concern, which is itself rooted in the maxim of Jesus: "You shall love the Lord your God with all your heart and with all your soul and with all your mind. This is the great and first commandment. And a second is like it: You shall love your neighbor as yourself. On these two commandments depend all the Law and the Prophets" (Matt 22:37–40; see also Mark 12:28–33). Heavenly-mindedness fixes our minds and hearts upon the twofold nature of this call to love ("a second is like it"), upon its priority on Godward love ("the great and first"), and on the seemingly global significance of its application ("on these two commandments depend all the Law and the Prophets").

Delight in the triune God does not displace concern for neighbor care and even enemy love. Timothy Jackson has analyzed ways in which "prudence, freedom, and justice" have led many to displace love from its position as first theology out of concern for what better seeks out and maintains care for human rights, dignity, and flourishing on the one hand, and lives conformed to the pattern of Jesus on the other hand.[64] Yet heavenly-mindedness actually sustains and motivates earthly action and fulfills the explicit teaching in word and deed offered by the Messiah about his own priorities.

Spirituality and social concern dare not be juxtaposed, though they must be sequenced. It was a spiritually saturated vision by which Dr. King summoned forth moral concern and called for social renewal.[65] We see this pairing illustrated week by week as congregants partake of the "gifts of God for the people of God" at the Lord's Supper before being sent with his blessing to love and do good works. That rhythm of divine-human fellowship

64. Timothy P. Jackson, *The Priority of Love: Christian Charity and Social Justice* (Princeton: Princeton University Press, 2003), 6.
65. See especially Martin Luther King Jr., "A Time to Break Silence," in *I Have a Dream: Writings and Speeches That Changed the World*, ed. James M. Washington (San Francisco: Harper San Francisco, 1992), 139–40.

prompting human service to neighbor exemplifies liturgically that deeper theological ordering of loves. Heavenly-mindedness grants a metaphysical and eschatological prioritization that prompts moral power, just as the sacramental partaking of the liturgy prepares us for a missional sending. Only as we are satisfied in that heavenly love and do lift up our hearts (*sursum corda*) unto the Lord alone will we be readied to enter into the fray of costly care for the least and the lost.

Heavenly-mindedness does not mark some esoteric fringe of Christian theology, then, but addresses the gospel nexus wherein the divine makes himself blessedly present unto the human and creaturely. My students are always struck by the pervasiveness of ascetical themes in reading through patristic literature, not only in texts or treatises overtly dealing with themes such as virginity or renunciation but also in unpacking the gifts and fruit of the Spirit, the Lord's Prayer, and the central tenets of the faith. Recovery of heavenly-mindedness in a world such as ours, marked by a seemingly claustrophobic creep of what Charles Taylor calls the "immanent frame," involves a recasting or recalibrating of the whole span of Christian doctrine and not simply a single supplement to an otherwise settled corpus. We do well to retrieve the classical, catholic commitment to heavenly-mindedness that was cherished also by the early Reformed and the later Puritans so that we might confess the whole faith in a way that manifests an ordered set of loves. As we do lift up our hearts in this way, drawing even our minds also to contemplate the heavenly, we may be more earnestly compelled to go out where Christ sends us.

4

Self-Denial

Reforming the Practices of Renunciation

For ancient Christians, asceticism did not represent a quadrant or portion of their intellectual or spiritual life. As recent historical scholarship has shown, asceticism tinged the fabric of their entire Christian existence under the sign of the cross.[1] While martyrdom might represent the fringe of this willful self-sacrifice, a vocation mercifully meant only for the few, the broader patterns of earthly renunciation marked the road of discipleship for all. To walk unto the sun was to flee the darkness. To journey toward heaven involved leaving behind the things of the earth.

1. Recent historiographic literature on asceticism in the Christian tradition has been marked fundamentally by two accounts: Michel Foucault, *The Uses of Pleasure*, vol. 2 of *The History of Sexuality*, trans. Robert Hurley (New York: Vintage, 1990), and vol. 3, *The Care of the Self*, trans. Robert Hurley (New York: Vintage, 1988); and Peter Brown, *The Body and Society: Men, Women, and Sexual Renunciation in Early Christianity* (New York: Columbia University Press, 1988). Brown has more recently turned from matters sexual to monetary as a nexus for both institutional and ascetical developments, especially in his *The Ransom of the Soul: Afterlife and Wealth in Early Western Christianity* (Cambridge, MA: Harvard University Press, 2015).

This chapter originally appeared in a slightly different form in Todd A. Wilson and Paul R. House, eds., *The Crucified Apostle: Essays on Paul and Peter* (Tübingen: Mohr Siebeck, 2017).

Asceticism, however, has endured a bumpy road throughout the Christian centuries. In the modern era, the Reformed tradition has viewed Christian asceticism with particular suspicion. None other than the great Dutch Reformed dogmatician Herman Bavinck characterizes it in these pejorative terms: "Basically, all asceticism is nothing other than self-willed religion. It consists in the accomplishment of a series of counsels that have not been enjoined by God but were instituted by human and ecclesiastical consent."[2] With these words, Herman Bavinck characterizes ascetical theology and practice as both materially and formally deficient: materially deficient in as much as it is "nothing other than self-willed religion"; formally deficient in that it is composed of a "series of counsels that . . . were instituted by human and ecclesiastical consent." In other words, asceticism contradicts the material principle of Reformed theology—*sola gratia*—as well as the formal principle of that tradition—*sola Scriptura*. Doubly indicted, it finds no comfort, much less encouragement, in his own theological project.

Fundamentally, Bavinck's concerns regarding those two principles are joined at the hip and united as one: *solus Christus*. To put the matter in the form of a question: does Christian asceticism really warrant the moniker "Christian" in theological and not just sociological terms? While it is patently obvious that thousands upon thousands have pursued pathways of ascetic discipline under the banner of Christianity, the question raised here addresses theological coherence. Does asceticism necessarily undercut the formal teaching authority of Jesus Christ as exercised through the instrument of Holy Scripture? And does asceticism essentially undermine the biblical insistence upon our fundamental need for grace over against the lurings of self-willed religion?

2. Herman Bavinck, *Holy Spirit, Church, and New Creation*, vol. 4 of *Reformed Dogmatics*, ed. John Bolt, trans. John Vriend (Grand Rapids: Baker Academic, 2008), 243.

In short, Bavinck's critique ultimately addresses not two discrete and disconnected matters but one complex matter: how does self-denial or ascetical practice relate to the person and work of the incarnate Son of God?

We will seek to respond to Bavinck's concern by considering the contours of what we will term evangelical asceticism. We will see the ways in which asceticism marked the faith and practice of the early Reformed movement, particularly as evident in the work of John Calvin. By considering the approach of Calvin to cast asceticism in the form of self-denial and, then, to govern it scripturally and locate it evangelically, we will be able to assess one detailed and influential example of Reformed asceticism. In so doing, we will see that Calvin demonstrates concern for both the formal and material principles raised much later by Bavinck, but Calvin articulates a pathway by which asceticism might be chastened, rather than rejected, by this reformational theology.

We will not be arguing that Calvin innovates in as yet unforeseen ways or that he is the apogee of evangelical asceticism. Long before, theologians ranging from Gregory to Basil to Augustine sought to relate the ascetic calling to the gift of Christ. In so doing, they believed they were being true not only to their vocation as bishops in the church but also to the exhortations of Holy Scripture. Though their theology of ascetic life was fashioned long before questions of authority and truth or of grace and salvation took the developed form that appeared in the time of the Protestant Reformation, this does not mean that patristic or medieval figures had nothing to say in this regard. And, of course, the Reformation must be appreciated as a long movement, and in many ways Calvin's project of evangelizing the ascetic impulse finds much fuller development in the project of the Puritan divines in the next century. In that movement, and in its Dutch equivalent, the *Nadere Reformatie*, one can observe Calvin's brief dogmatic sketch being expanded with greater specificity and vibrancy.

These historical limits to our inquiry notwithstanding, we press on to consider the dogmatic sketch of evangelical asceticism presented in Calvin's *Institutes of the Christian Religion*. We do so in the belief that the Reformed movement was meant to be a renewal rather than a repudiation of the Christian tradition of faith and practice. While many facets of ecclesial life would be identified as mere custom, not genuine tradition, and thus excised, Calvin and the early Reformed tradition showed a keen eye in observing the fundamentally scriptural roots of Christian asceticism in the teaching and the life of Jesus Christ and his apostles. Not only that, however, but they also sought to better relate that ascetical concern to the doctrines of Christ and his gospel and of Christ and his rule so that asceticism would ever be chastened by the doctrines of grace and of Holy Scripture. In that regard, we sketch not only a commitment to retain or recover Christian asceticism but also, more fundamentally, a concern to understand its shape and contours in such a manner that it can be termed evangelical asceticism.

The Contexts and Definition of Ascetical Theology

Before considering ways in which self-denial might be construed as an evangelical asceticism, we do well to consider the definition of asceticism itself and then to turn to its moral and ontological context. How do we define asceticism? Scholars of late antiquity in its pagan, Jewish, or Christian forms continue to debate this. Perhaps the following definition covers terrain broadly enough so as to be relatively uncontroversial. According to Steven Fraade, asceticism has "two main components: (1) the exercise of disciplined effort toward the goal of spiritual perfection (however understood), which requires (2) abstention (whether total or partial, permanent or temporary, individualistic or communalistic) from the satisfaction of otherwise permitted earthly, creaturely desires."[3] Asceticism involves both pull and push based on a desired benefit and a necessary cost and, thus, cannot be reduced to any painstaking discipline. While the benefits or blessings might be construed in many different ways, their transcendent character marks off asceticism from mere physical discipline (along the lines of dieting or athletic training).[4]

Asceticism was not and is not the exclusive property of the Christian tradition. Religious traditions of late antiquity as well as the philosophical way of *paideia* involved ascetical facets or aspects in their undertaking.[5] In considering the way that reformational theology (as developed in the sixteenth century) might recontextualize Christian asceticism, we are engaging in a second step of reform, for patristic thinkers had long before sought to express ways in which asceticism might be practiced by Christians vis-à-vis their pagan counterparts.

Recent scholarship on late antique renunciation has emphasized the bodily and the social facets of asceticism. In so doing they have complicated an older portrayal of its roots, which had long been identified with Platonic or Middle Platonic dualism. In that story, a strong material-immaterial dualism paired with a metaphysical hierarchy that privileged the form over matter led to an ethic of renunciation, whereby the human sought to flee this wretched flesh for the realm of the disembodied spirit (at least as much as possible in this earthly life). But Peter Brown has shown that early Christian renunciation was wrought out of a high valuation of the body, not a low estimate of its dignity and signifi-

---

3. Steven D. Fraade, "Ascetical Aspects of Ancient Judaism," in *Jewish Spirituality*, ed. A. Green (New York: Crossroad, 1986), 257 (253–88).

4. Gavin Flood, *The Ascetic Self: Subjectivity, Memory, and Tradition* (Cambridge: Cambridge University Press, 2004), 216–17.

5. Paul Rabbow, *Seelenführung: Methodik der Exerzitien in der Antike* (Munich: Kösel, 1954); Pierre Hadot, *Exercices spirituels et philosophie antique*, 2nd ed. (Paris: Etudes augustiniennes, 1981); Pierre Hadot, *La philosophie comme manière de vivre* (Paris: Albin Michel, 2001).

cance.[6] Asceticism in the Christian world flowed from a serious consideration of the gravity of the body paired with an obedience to the warning of Christ that one cannot serve two masters and, thus, one must offer single-minded or single-hearted devotion unto God. Christian asceticism involves bodily renunciation of certain earthly goods or pleasures, yet in so doing it need not flow from any hatred of or even dismissal of the body as itself a good.

Christian asceticism has also been recategorized as a social phenomenon. For too long asceticism was viewed as the domain of the monk and nun, and hence it was viewed as a reclusive calling. Recent historiography has complexified this matter in two ways. First, we see that while the monastic practice probably arises earlier than had previously been thought, it also takes forms that are far more socially interconnected than the reclusive approach would suggest.[7] Again, Peter Brown has played a pivotal role in observing the way in which Christian asceticism was bound up with a new polity wherein the city and its natural order was no longer the ultimate arbiter of values and practices to be manifested by bodies; rather, a new city of spiritual substance was viewed as the transcendent source of bodily valuation and discipline.[8] Second, and more fundamentally, ascetical practice was never viewed as the exclusive calling of the religious orders but as a universal expectation (in various forms and degrees) for all Christian men and women. This understanding has effects on the ways in which we might receive Calvin's correctives regarding asceticism. Whereas Matthew Myer Boulton has argued at length that Calvin sought to democratize or, perhaps better put, univer-

6. Brown, *The Body and Society*, 425.

7. On the development of monasticism, see Samuel Rubenson, "Christian Asceticism and the Emergence of the Monastic Tradition," in *Asceticism*, ed. Vincent L. Wimbush and Richard Valantasis (New York: Oxford University Press, 1995), 49–57. For claims that monasticism arose in the apostolic era, see J. C. O'Neill, "The Origins of Monasticism," in *The Making of Orthodoxy*, ed. Rowan Williams (Cambridge: Cambridge University Press, 1989), 270–87.

8. Brown, *The Body and Society*, 436–37.

salize monasticism in Geneva by rendering its essential commitments and practices capable of participation by all Christian men and women, we might better substitute the term "asceticism" for "monasticism."[9] Calvin addresses self-denial as an evangelical understanding of and universal demand for Christian asceticism, but he does not in any way suggest that monasticism as such bears such an evangelical interpretation, much less an extensive demand for participation. Awareness of developments in the history of asceticism in late antiquity keeps us alert to the possibility of a non-monastic asceticism that Calvin is addressing.

A cluster of terms arise in the realm of ascetics: "renunciation," "self-denial," "mortification," and "contempt for the world" (*contemptus mundi*). While these terms and their related images may appear in a whole host of ascetical discourses, markedly different moral ontologies lie underneath this diaspora of ethical and ascetical projects. As seen above, the patristic theologians sought to distance their own reflections from various pagan asceticisms; for example, Augustine would develop his writings on perfection, continence, virginity, and marriage in the wake of the Manichean challenge. And further recalibration to the Christian moral ontology underlying its ascetics of discipleship would be prompted by the early Reformed movement's emphasis upon Christ, grace, and faith with regard to salvation and the Christian life. Remembering that asceticism is not simply the practice of excruciating self-discipline but is always paired with a line of thinking or desiring that is fixed upon some transcendent goal, what we might call an eschatology of one sort or another, we do well to inquire not only and not even primarily into its practical shape but into its doctrinal moorings or dogmatic architecture.[10]

9. Matthew Myer Boulton, *Life in God: John Calvin, Practical Formation, and the Future of Protestant Theology* (Grand Rapids: Eerdmans, 2011).

10. For assessments of this dogmatic architecture or moral ontology in patristic theology, see T. H. J. van Eijk, "Marriage and Virginity, Death and Immortality," in *Epektasis*, ed. J. Fontaine and C. Kannengiesser (Paris:

What are the coordinated beliefs regarding the self, sin, redemption, and, most significant of all, the transcendent that impinge upon and shape the space for this ascetic practice?

The Shape of Evangelical Asceticism: Self-Denial

In recent years Gavin Flood has asked whether ascetic discipline might be a gift of God.[11] The question is not a new one and may serve as a helpful prompt for considering the way in which John Calvin received and revived the ascetic tradition. His greatest concern as a theologian and pastor was to conceive of practices of self-denial and of renunciation of worldly things in a manner that located these endeavors within the good news of Jesus Christ. Calvin did not merely want to describe such endeavors as a response to the gospel of Christ that is nonetheless distinct from the gospel; rather, he sought to locate them within the repentance and renewal that the gospel itself brings and a crucial facet of the second element of the double grace in Christ. To grasp this reorienting of ascetical practice around the person and work of Christ, we do well first to attend to the structural moves made by Calvin in addressing ascetics.

The topics of self-denial and renunciation appear in book 3 of Calvin's *Institutes of the Christian Religion*.[12] There he addresses "the way in which we receive the grace of Christ: what benefits come to us from it, and what effects follow." The whole book is prompted by the observation that "as long as Christ remains outside of us, and we are separated from him, all that he has suffered

Beauchesne, 1972), 209–35; and especially John Behr, *Asceticism and Anthropology in Irenaeus and Clement*, Oxford Early Christian Studies (New York: Oxford University Press, 2000).

11. Flood, *The Ascetic Self*, xi.

12. John Calvin, *Institutes of the Christian Religion*, ed. John T. McNeill, trans. Ford Lewis Battles, Library of Christian Classics 20 (Louisville: Westminster John Knox, 2006). Future references to this work are noted in the text in parentheses.

and done for the salvation of the human race remains useless and of no value for us" (III.i.1). Having just concluded his discussion of the person and narrative of Christ—the gospel story—Calvin is making a pointed qualification: this remains but a fascinating and exceptional story of late antiquity, of a life long ago in a land far away, unless we are somehow united to Christ. Calvin then launches into his famed doctrine of union with Christ by the Holy Spirit, who is the "bond by which Christ effectually unites us to himself" (III.i.1).

Calvin spoke of the use and value of Christ for us in his introduction to book 3. Soon thereafter he traces out this blessing in a twofold manner. "With good reason, the sum of the gospel is held to consist in repentance and forgiveness of sins [Luke 24:47; Acts 5:31]. . . . Now, both repentance and forgiveness of sins—that is, newness of life and free reconciliation—are conferred on us by Christ, and both are attained by us through faith" (III.iii.1). Here language of a double grace (*duplex gratia*) is suggested for the first time, to be noted again (III.xi.1). Traditionally, interpreters have rendered his distinction as being between justification and sanctification. While fully appropriate, it is worth noting that Calvin uses neither word as his leading descriptor of the twofold gift here. He instead prefers to lead with the biblical language of repentance and of the forgiveness of sins and then to add overlapping or even synonymous terms (such as "regeneration" and "reconciliation" or "justification"). His broad point, however, and the very reason for making the distinction is to remind his reader that both are gifts or graces and, as such, are a part of the gospel promise of Jesus. Calvin takes this judgment to be plain from his repeated scriptural citations (in Luke 24:47 and Acts 5:31).

Two major moves are made here that locate ascetical activity within the promise of the gospel. First, Calvin defines repentance neither as a preparation for the gospel nor as a distinct response to the gospel but as a divine provision of the gospel that takes the form of sanctified human action. His reading of Jesus's scriptural message relayed in Luke 24:47 locates repentance as a believer's action flowing from and gifted by God's kindness. While repentance is our action, its existence flows from God's good promise, indeed, it is a part of that promise, not as a condition but as a creation flowing from the unconditioned gift of Christ. Second, the reformer then locates self-denial and renunciation within the category of repentance or sanctification, employing the terminology of mortification and vivification to do so. Calvin makes plain that he is aware of entering a massive field of study when addressing the Christian life: "In composing exhortations on but a single virtue, the ancient doctors, as we see, became very prolix. Yet in this they waste no words." He notes that assessment of any one virtue leads to addressing a slew of interrelated matters. Such is not his goal or purpose. "I do not intend to develop here, the instruction in living that I am now about to offer to the point of describing individual virtues at length, and of digressing into exhortations. Such may be sought from others' writings, especially from the homilies of the fathers." Calvin plainly observes the nature of the patristic approach to ascetical and virtue ethics and commends their exhortations, seeing no need to replace them. What will he add? "To show the godly man how he may be directed to a rightly ordered life, and briefly to set down some universal rule with which to determine his duties—this will be quite enough for me" (III.vi.1). While we will return to the issue of rules, regulation, and the determination of one's duties in our next section (addressing ways in which Calvin recalibrated ascetical theology along the lines of the Reformed Scripture principle), here we should expand on the ways in which he addresses an appropriate direction unto this life and what it means for it to be "rightly ordered."

Strictly speaking, Calvin's treatise on ascetical theology or what he calls the "sum of the Christian life" runs from chapters 6 through 10 of book 3. Yet Calvin has already begun to address the life of repentance beginning in chapters 2 through 5. Here he has defined faith (ch. 2) and repentance (ch. 3). Next, he deconstructs later accretions to repentance that marred the sacramental-penitential system of the medieval church by construing repentance as something that satisfies God (ch. 4) or by supplementing repentance with indulgences and other rites rooted in nothing more than human tradition (ch. 5). Having made these basic dogmatic moves (in chs. 2–3) and cleared the ground of so much ballast (in chs. 4–5), Calvin now turns to address the life of the Christian and scriptural motivations thereunto (ch. 6).

The lure of self-denial flows from a greater good, a future good that outweighs and outstrips the fleeting and faint allures of this present age. Calvin refers to this greater good as the "true fountain" of Jesus Christ himself (III.vi.3). He explains how the various benefits enjoyed in union with Christ not only objectively mark us out before God but also call forth a corresponding subjective action or moral movement:

> Ever since God revealed himself Father to us, we must prove our ungratefulness to him if we did not in turn show ourselves his sons [Mal. 1:6; Eph. 5:1; 1 John 3:1]. Ever since Christ cleansed us with the washing of his blood, and imparted this cleansing through baptism, it would be unfitting to befoul ourselves with new pollutions [Eph. 5:26; Heb. 10:10; 1 Cor. 6:11; 1 Peter 1:15,19]. Ever since he engrafted us into his body, we must take especial care not to disfigure ourselves, who are his members, with any spot or blemish [Eph. 5:23–33; 1 Cor. 6:15; John 15:3–6]. Ever since Christ himself, who is our head, ascended into heaven, it behooves us, having laid aside love of earthly things, wholeheartedly to aspire heavenward [Col. 3:1ff.]. Ever since the Holy Spirit dedicated us as temples to God, we must take care that God's glory shine through us, and must not commit anything to defile ourselves with the filthiness of sin [1 Cor. 3:16; 6:19; 2 Cor. 6:16]. Ever since both our souls and bodies

were destined for heavenly incorruption and an unfading crown [1 Peter 5:4], we ought to strive manfully to keep them pure and uncorrupted until the day of the Lord [1 Thess. 5:23; cf. Phil. 1:10]. (III.vi.3)

Calvin explicitly notes that philosophers who commend virtue can only and do only rise to call for action based on the "natural dignity of man," whereas he suggests that a supernatural dignity conferred upon humanity in Christ offers a greater moral theology.

What is the shape of this Christian life of faith and repentance, of this journey marked by the gift of God and the resulting agency of his adopted sons and daughters? If justification really comes to the ungodly, what can and does Calvin say of the sanctification given to them as well? In chapter 7, he focuses upon self-denial as the sum of the Christian life. He employs language of sacrifice, transformation, and conformity unto God (not the world) to describe this rhythm of self-denial. A lengthy quotation offers his most pertinent comments on the matter:

If we, then, are not our own [cf. 1 Cor. 6:19] but the Lord's, it is clear what error we must flee, and whither we must direct all the acts of our life.

We are not our own: let not our reason nor our will, therefore, sway our plans and deeds. We are not our own: let us therefore not set it as our goal to seek what is expedient for us according to the flesh. We are not our own: in so far as we can, let us therefore forget ourselves and all that is ours.

Conversely, we are God's: let us therefore live for him and die for him. We are God's: let his wisdom and will therefore rule all our actions. We are God's: let all the parts of our life accordingly strive toward him as our only lawful goal [Rom. 14:8; cf. 1 Cor. 6:19]. O, how much has

that man profited who, having been taught that he is not
his own, has taken away dominion and rule from his own
reason that he may yield it to God! For, as consulting our
self-interest is the pestilence that most effectively leads
to our destruction, so the sole haven of salvation is to be
wise in nothing and to will nothing through ourselves
but to follow the leading of the Lord alone.

Let this therefore be the first step, that a man depart
from himself in order that he may apply the whole force
of his ability in the service of the Lord. (III.vii.1)

Calvin locates self-denial within the matrix of creation by the triune God—the covenant with the Father of Israel, the union with Christ, and the indwelling of the Holy Spirit. In other words, the renunciation of self-possession expressed here makes sense only amidst a transcendent claim of possession by the triune God of grace.

These remarks about "departing from himself" are for the sake of the "service of the Lord"; interpreting his focus requires attending to his exegetical sources, in particular Romans 12:1-2, wherein offering one's spiritual worship unto the Lord (which Paul identifies as one's whole self) requires a transformation of the mind, a renewal that requires nonconformity to the ways of the world and regeneration of the ways within the natural self.

Romans 12 prefaces this call to sacrifice and worship and transformation of the self with reference to the "mercies of God," assumedly the glorious truths relayed in chapters 1 through 11 that precede this portion of Holy Scripture. Calvin makes much of this order, noting that the repentance described at such length not only in these verses but more broadly in Romans 12-15 flows from faith.[13] In other words, evangelical asceticism will be prompted

13. For helpful analysis of the fundamental significance of Romans
12:1-2 in Calvin's description of self-denial, see Randall C. Zachman, "'Deny

forward by eschatological hope rather than prodded by a bygone simplicity or primordial innocence.[14] Repeatedly, Calvin returns to the language of "devotion to God" as the motivating source of self-denial (III.vii.2, 8). Devotion does not describe one's faithfulness to God in a way that benefits God; rather, devotion unto God, for Calvin, is the kind of devotion expressed by a dependent. Hence Calvin concludes his description of self-denial with a lengthy analysis of how trusting God's blessing frees one from the fear and anxiety of being one's own master and Lord; in other words, devotion to this God takes the form of trust in his provision through Jesus Christ, and that trust invariably moves us out of ourselves and refocuses us upon God as our compass, our sun, and our Savior.

It is worth noting that this observation regarding the root of self-denial in faith is not unique to the Protestant tradition. Maximus the Confessor linked the spiritual war against the flesh with faith:

> Now perhaps someone will say: I have faith and faith in Him is enough for me for salvation. But James contradicts him, saying: The devils also believe and tremble; and again: Faith without works is dead in itself, as also the works without faith. In what manner then do we believe in Him? Is it that we believe Him about future things, but about transient and present things do not believe Him, and are therefore immersed in material things and live in the flesh, and battle against the Spirit? But those who truly believed Christ and, through the commandments, made Him to dwell wholly within themselves spoke in

Yourself and Take Up Your Cross': John Calvin on the Christian Life," *International Journal of Systematic Theology* 11, no. 4 (2009): 471 (466–80).

14. See, e.g., Irenaeus's *Against Heresies* 3.22–23, and *On the Apostolic Preaching* 11–16, as well as the commentary of Behr, *Asceticism and Anthropology*, 49n51.

this fashion: And I live, now not I; but Christ liveth in me. And that I live in the flesh: I live in the faith of the Son of God, who loved me, and delivered Himself for me.[15]

There are precursors to evangelical asceticism, then, though the systemic emphasis upon the order of faith and repentance and of justification and sanctification is highlighted by Calvin with such force because of late medieval practices that had undercut classical Christian discipleship.

Calvin then addresses cross-bearing as a fundamental description of the Christian life (ch. 8). Because the Christian life involves union with Christ—with his person, story, and benefits—the experience of cross-bearing in the present comes as part of the package, as it were. Suffering in the present marks the life of every Christian. Calvin describes the experience of suffering in various ways: as training and instruction for the spiritually immature and unperfected (III.viii.4), as testing for the weak (III.viii.4), as medicine for the spiritually ill (III.viii.5), and as fatherly discipline for God's children (III.viii.6). How is it these things? It is because suffering in the present is accompanied with the gift of hope in the faithfulness and provision of God (III.viii.3, 8). Calvin expressly condemns stoicism and notes that the patient endurance to which Christ calls his people is not without sorrow and, thus, cannot be undertaken without anguish, passion, and pain (III.viii.9–10).

Amidst that insistence upon suffering in the present life, Calvin reattunes us to the broader shape of history by pointing again to our future life, and more specifically to the need to meditate upon the eternal life that will be ours in Christ (ch. 9). "If heaven is our homeland, what else is the earth but our place of

15. "The Ascetic Life," in *The Ascetic Life and the Four Centuries*, Ancient Christian Writers 21, trans. Polycarp Sherwood (New York: Newman, 1956), 123 (section 34).

exile?" (III.ix.4). Calvin regularly employs the language of the pilgrimage or the exodus to describe the life of the Christian. The trick—and this is not an easy matter—is to "let believers accustom themselves to a contempt of the present life that engenders no hatred of it or ingratitude against God" (III.ix.3). In other words, contempt for the present flows from the excessive good of the future, not from any inherent ill in the current moment. The present is not enough, but that does not mean that it is not good, that it is not from God, or that it is not to be received with gratitude. Nevertheless, just as faith and repentance are paired realities (like the "returning and rest" that the prophet Isaiah spoke of in Isa 30:15), so a contempt for the present and a desire for the future are twinned human experiences.

Then Calvin returns from that account of eschatology and meditation upon eternity to reconsider the present and what he deems our "use of the present life and its helps" (ch. 10). "Let this be our principle: that the use of God's gifts is not wrongly directed when it is referred to that end to which the Author himself created and destined them for us, since he created them for our good, not for our ruin" (III.x.2). So the manner of employing earthly goods flows from both their creation and their "end" to which God has "destined them for us." His ethic is neither merely creational nor solely eschatological but relates the two and, thus, locates present use amidst past creation and future destiny. As to extent, Calvin repeatedly uses the language of moderation, frugality, and sobriety (see, e.g., III.x.5). He also notes that there are various "callings" (vocations). Over against "the judgment of human and philosophical reason," which would reduce all ethics to a universal or homogenous form, Calvin insists that God diversifies his gifts and his callings, and we dare not constrict his direction. Again, this is why Romans 12:2 speaks of the need for a renewed mind to exercise discernment about the true, good, and beautiful, precisely because self-denial never takes the form of a shoehorn and always involves personal dispossession of oneself and equally personal dependence upon the prompting of God.

As we sum up Calvin's description of the space for self-denial, the first thing to note must be its Christological location: in union with Christ, as part of the promise of the gospel, we are led away from ourselves and led further into life in Christ. Further, this process of self-denial plays out in the course of an ongoing history, and it is prompted both by faith in God's blessing and by meditation upon our eternal bliss, rooted in divine faithfulness in the past (both in the singular works of Christ in the first century and in the previous personal deliverances of God's Spirit to us in our own lifetime), and performed amidst the tumult of our present pilgrimmage to our heavenly end.

The Standards of Evangelical Asceticism: Scriptural Exhortations to Self-Denial

Herman Bavinck says that "the New Testament does not first of all recommend the virtues that enable believers to conquer the world but, while it bids them avoid all false asceticism (Rom 14:14; 1 Tim 4:4–5; Titus 1:15), lists as fruits of the Spirit the virtues of 'love, joy, peace, patience, kindness, generosity, faithfulness, gentleness, and self-control' (Gal 5:22–23; Eph 4:32; 1 Thess 5:14ff.; 1 Pet 3:8ff.; 2 Pet 1:5–7; 1 John 2:15)."[16] We have seen that John Calvin did not juxtapose asceticism or virtue ethics from scriptural teaching on the fruit of the Spirit as does Bavinck. As observed above, Calvin endorsed the teaching of the fathers regarding particular virtues and exhortations unto renunciation; he only desired to provide an appropriate theological order to direct the way in which Christians pursue such moral endeavors.

16. Bavinck, *Reformed Dogmatics*, 4:674.

Remember that Calvin insisted that self-denial must be governed by looking to God in all things.[17] This marks some of his criticism of monastic practices (which also focus on self-denial). For centuries, Christian theologians had made a distinction between commands and counsels (see Thomas, *Summa theologiae*, Ia-IIae.108.4): while commands are given by God and applicable to all Christians, counsels are wise maxims that are binding only on a select few (e.g., celibacy is advised by Paul and followed by the monks). Two major differences can be seen between this approach and that of Calvin: (1) Calvin believes self-denial is universally binding upon all Christians; and (2) Calvin believes that self-denial is to be governed by "looking to God in all things" through Holy Scripture, and he does not believe that "counsels" of Scripture should be made binding on any subsection of the church unless Scripture expressly does so itself. His comments on 1 Corinthians 7:8 are indicative of this dynamic: while gifts of celibacy are given to some, they are not to be enforced on any. Calvin will venture arguments that earlier monastic lifestyles (as advocated by Augustine or, we might add, Athanasius) were far more in line with scriptural teaching than those of contemporary monastics, for ancient monastic communities were more integrated into the wider life of the congregation (e.g., IV.xiii.9, 14). Calvin notes that later monastic practices made it impossible for a monk to also serve well as a priest because the one called for withdrawal from society while the other demanded immersion within the community (IV.v.8). In so doing he is drawing on observations made by Pope Gregory the Great himself, who had said that "no one can properly be both a monk and a cleric."[18]

17. See further his comments on 2 Corinthians 1:9: "We must begin by despairing of ourselves but only in order that we may hope in God; we must be brought low in ourselves but only in order that we may be raised up by his power."

18. On Calvin and monasticism, see David Steinmetz, "Calvin and the Monastic Ideal," in *Calvin in Context* (New York: Oxford University Press, 1995), 187–98.

What we see in these concerns is a formal disagreement regarding the proper authority that governs our moral and ascetical practice. Whereas a twofold authority structure had developed, with universal commands given by God and specific counsels given by various figures within the ecclesiastical hierarchy, Calvin argues that all ecclesial authority is ministerial in nature and is thus tethered to the enscripturated Word of God. All Christians are bound so far as Holy Scripture speaks regarding self-denial and their renunciation of earthly things for heavenly good. However, in so far as the writings of the prophets and apostles remain silent, so the church must do so as well. An individual Christian may discern something wise or prudent to undertake beyond the explicit prompting or directive of the Bible, of course, and it is to be expected that such judgments will occur across the board. However, the ministers of the church are not to purport to make such judgments *in loco parentis* or with any binding authority.

Calvin does not merely bring up scriptural authority to deconstruct medieval Roman customs that he deems illegitimate or extra-biblical. He also wants to reorient his reader to areas of biblical emphasis regarding self-denial, chief among them being the Sabbath practices of the people of God. As he says elsewhere, "the Lord the more frequently testifies that he had given, in the Sabbath, a symbol of sanctification to his ancient people."[19] In keeping the Sabbath, believers refocus their time and all their investments (of energy and capital) upon God and also refocus the time of any within their household or influence similarly. Sabbath keeping marks the classical Reformed tradition in a way unprecedented in Christian history. A simplicity and coherence of principle mark its development in both its (in some ways quite different) continental and Puritan forms as they developed in the late sixteenth and early seventeenth centuries.

19. John Calvin, *Commentaries on the First Book of Moses Called Genesis*, vol. 1, trans. John King (Grand Rapids: Eerdmans, 1948), 106 (on Gen 2:3).

Calvin and the classical Reformed tradition's focus upon the Sabbath and paired critique of Roman and later Anglican celebration of a lush liturgical calendar flow from a common fount. The Reformed tradition does not derive its temporal order or its polemical commentary on other traditions' use of calendars from any anti-religious animus. Rather, Sabbath keeping demonstrates an assumed principle regarding the way that temporal habits and rhythmic practices of spiritual consequence form the people of God. But such habits and practices do so in as much as they draw us out of ourselves, and, therefore, they must be mandated from above, rather than imagined from our own vanity.

Evangelical Asceticism:
Recovering and Reforming Self-Denial

Interestingly, the single most excerpted portion of Calvin's *Institutes* through the centuries has been this portion of book 3 wherein he addresses the topics of self-denial and the proper use of earthly goods. It has been circulating under the title *The Golden Booklet of the Christian Life*. Today, however, the heavy influence of neo-Calvinism or Kuyperianism and of the Weberian and Niebuhrian approaches to reflecting upon the sociological, economic, and cultural significance of Calvinism has led to an image of the reformers' theology that rarely, if ever, finds itself identified with heavenly-mindedness, self-denial, contentment, Sabbath, and renunciation of the world.

Indeed, one of the reasons for Calvinism's cultural caché in the modern Western world has been its supposed valuation of this world as dignified, glorious, and worthy of our endeavors. This-worldly spirituality has been most potently demonstrated in the fiction of Reformed author Marilynne Robinson, especially in her Pulitzer Prize–winning *Gilead*, wherein we read that "all the world is lit up like transfiguration."[20] Corresponding to this vision of the world has been an approach to work, in which Reformed theology in the twentieth century has expanded on the doctrine of vocation in a way that has brought coherence and vibrancy to Christian approaches to a whole host of topics, ranging from finance and sexuality to politics and education. Because of its eschatological opposition to dispensationalism since the late nineteenth century, Reformed theology has sought to emphasize that while a dismissiveness or denigration of the world may flow from a rapture theology, a holistic eschatology (as sketched so forcibly, for example, by Bavinck) presents a much richer basis for investing one's capital (in every sense) in worldly betterment. Thus, it is standard fare for churches influenced by this stream of Kuyperian thought to identify their mission (as have two of my own churches) to benefit the city spiritually, socially, and culturally.

My emphasis here ought not be mistaken for a rejection of this Kuyperian or neo-Calvinist vision of Christ as Lord of all things, the sovereign over every sphere of life. Nor do I wish to deny, in any sense, that we are to glorify God in all we do, seeking to act out of faith according to his Word and unto his glory. That said, there are serious dangers to this emphasis, chief among them a loss of proportion. Culture in its various forms can be a good, but even at its very best it can only be a secondary, participating good that pales in comparison to our primary good: the triune God who participates in no one, but who may be participated in by those united to him through Jesus Christ. In seeking not to deny the wide reach of God's blessing, modern Reformed theology has too frequently failed to honor, or has even blatantly denigrated, the bliss of God.

We must go one step further, however, and note that it is not merely that there has been a failure of eschatology and a

---

20. Marilynne Robinson, *Gilead* (New York: Farrar, Straus, and Giroux, 2003), 245. Her protagonist in this volume, the Rev. John Ames, channels the theology of Calvin and Barth directly, in particular regarding the holiness of the ordinary.

truncation of Christian hope. While necessary as an assessment, that judgment is not sufficient to steer the ship aright. An ethical anemia has also set in owing to that eschatological thinness. When we consider Calvin, however, we observe a thick description of the Christian life that is rooted in more than mere gratitude, command, or response. Calvin locates the life of renewal, regeneration, and repentance in the wider orbit of the gospel itself, and he addresses the two key ordering questions that attend consideration of that calling. "Now this Scriptural instruction of which we speak has two main aspects. The first is that the love of righteousness, to which we are otherwise not at all inclined by nature, may be instilled and established in our hearts; the second, that a rule be set forth for us that does not let us wander about in our zeal for righteousness" (*Institutes* III.vi.2). We have sought to appreciate the way in which his reformational theology of grace and of the Scripture principle has reoriented his commitment to the moral theology of the Christian past, especially in its ascetical demands. He endorses the same virtues and exhortations (even in their patristic form) but wants to provide a new order to direct the way in which we approach their practice.

We might conclude by directing a contemporary question and asking whether Calvin's account can provide a reasonable response. Eugene Rogers objects to the use of the term "self-denial" in describing Christian ascesis, pointing out that it makes no sense to call something the "denial" of the self when it actually entails the development of true personhood in relationship to God.[21] Why, then, does Calvin speak of self-denial when addressing the Christian life or process of sanctification? The immediate answer is that language of self-denial comes from Holy Scripture (so Luke 9:23). Christians may query whether such terminology ought to

21. Cited in Nathan Jennings, *Theology as Ascetic Act: Disciplining Christian Discourse*, American University Studies in Theology and Religion 307 (New York: Peter Lang, 2010), 15n67.

hold significant sway or significance in our broader moral theology and in what terms it might be properly understood, but they cannot very well question its employment as such. Let us refine our question, then, and ask why "self-denial" is a significant term for an evangelical asceticism or a Reformed moral theology and, if it is significant, how it might be governed by wider thinking about the God of the gospel and the creaturely order that this Lord has brought into being in Christ.

When speaking of asceticism, one speaks of the self. But to make this observation is only to begin to query the character of asceticism and the contours of its practice, rather than to foreclose or conclude such an investigation. Speech about the self itself is conflicted, not only in Holy Scripture but also in the Christian tradition. We are to love the self and pattern our love of others along our love of self (so Jesus's rendition of the second great commandment), and yet love of the self is viewed as a detrimental and evil practice. The later Christian tradition has spoken of self-love in this complex, multi-form fashion as well, in so doing gesturing toward the complexity of Holy Scripture itself.[22] Can we say more about the nature of such an asceticism? Gleaning from Calvin, I think four facets might be summarized as significant for shaping a distinctly evangelical approach to self-denial.

First, Christian asceticism is not merely or even primarily about contempt for the world as such. Any notion of *contemptus mundi* that is to prove serviceable to the gospel must be coordinated with a contempt for the self. The world as such, and its moral nature, flows from the way in which it is engaged by human creatures before God. Thus, riches or poverty may be received rightly or wrongly, depending upon the posture with which one possesses that much or that little.

22. The pivotal study of this multi-form reality continues to be Oliver O'Donovan, *The Problem of Self-Love in St. Augustine* (New Haven: Yale University Press, 1980).

Second, Christian asceticism is not merely or even primarily about contempt at all. First and foremost, contempt of the world and of the self must be preceded by delight in the good things of life: God and all things in as much as they participate in God's bliss and blessing. In commenting upon 2 Corinthians 2:14, Calvin insists: "the only way to make right progress in the Gospel is to be attracted by the sweet fragrance of Christ so that we desire Him enough to bid the enticements of the world farewell." Hence, present restraint (as described in *Institutes* III.x) must be fueled by meditation upon future blessing (as described in the immediately preceding section: III.ix). And present restraint may not take the form of hatred of the world as a good; indeed, Christians must be able to delight in the goods of the world.[23]

Third, Christian asceticism must be located among the creaturely coordinates of the gospel, namely, the resonances that echo back upon and press forward into the reception of grace by those enfolded within his identity. So any call to denial or renunciation is a temporal reality and makes sense only in a particular historic frame of reference: the pilgrim avoids enjoying the route, however scenic it may be, to any extent that would lead him away from yearning for his final destination. Similarly, the Christian contents herself with God's provisions for the day and avoids fostering a yearning for greater earthly good, lest she forget the heavenly satisfactions that await her in glory. Christians do live in a state of grace, so that there are temporal goods to be enjoyed; Christians are not yet in the state of glory, so they must expect to experience delayed gratification. "Since the eternal inheritance of man is in heaven, it is truly right that we should tend thither; yet must we fix our foot on earth long enough to enable us to consider the abode which God requires man to use for a time. For we are now

23. Calvin offers a comparative reading of 2 Corinthians 1:12 and 10:17 (in his commentary) to address ways in which Paul can singularly glory in God while also glorying in goods provided by God.

conversant with that history which teaches us that Adam was, by divine appointment, an inhabitant of the earth, in order that he might, in passing through his earthly life, meditate on heavenly glory."[24]

Fourth, Christian asceticism will be guided by the church's authoritative teaching of Holy Scripture (only) in so far as the Scriptures do speak and then by the discernment of individual consciences shaped by that scriptural revelation. Thus emphasis will be placed upon practices such as keeping the Sabbath holy, the giving of tithes and offerings, and occasional fasting, which find explicit warrant in God's Word. Still further, prayer remains the most profound ascetic practice and is not only commanded but exemplified and illustrated throughout the Scriptures. In prayer, Christians turn from their restless activity to rest their anxieties and needs, their aspirations and joys, their very selves, upon God. While individuals and families may opt to include other rites or rhythms in their spiritual practice from time to time and with regard to varying challenges or callings, church communities will focus upon these scripturally warranted practices in their discipleship.[25]

More could surely be said about Christian asceticism, especially with regard to particular virtues or habits that might be explored in detail. As with Calvin, we have avoided any lengthy analysis of particular examples, believing that the fundamental need of the day is again a matter of order and direction. We show how asceticism functions as a part of evangelical faith and practice in the Reformed tradition and helps reimagine a more spiritual view of the Christian life this side of the Kuyperian turn. We do so, hopefully, without losing the earthiness and extent of that vision

24. Calvin, *Commentaries on the First Book of Moses Called Genesis*, 1:114–15.

25. For example, Calvin has much to say regarding wisdom for ministers with regard to renunciation of earthly goods and of one's own self in the exercise of their pastoral office (see, e.g., *Commentary on 2 Corinthians* 13:7).

of sanctification. The good news of Jesus does come to men and women in this earth; the good news involves the promise that God will draw them away from themselves and will draw them unto his heavenly presence (which will eventually fill the whole earth). This good news is God's doing and so is a promise; this good news brings our transformation and so brings ethical activity. While the evangelical word does not depend upon or condition itself upon our willful self-denial, the word brings hope because it does assure us that God will lead us outside ourselves and into the posture of receiving life more richly from him.

EPILOGUE

*Brothers, join in imitating me, and keep your eyes on those who walk
according to the example you have in us. For many, of whom I have
often told you and now tell you even with tears, walk as enemies of the
cross of Christ. Their end is destruction, their god is their belly, and
they glory in their shame, with minds set on earthly things. But our
citizenship is in heaven, and from it we await a Savior, the Lord Jesus
Christ, who will transform our lowly body to be like his glorious body,
by the power that enables him even to subject all things to himself.
Therefore, my brothers, whom I love and long for, my joy and crown,
stand firm thus in the Lord, my beloved.*

—Philippians 3:17–4:1 (ESV)

When I began research on patristic and Puritan ascetical theology, I never imagined myself being rushed to an emergency room
with great haste nor of residing in a hospital at length, undergo-
ing major surgery, and being diagnosed with a chronic and severe
condition. As it turns out, study of these themes and texts proved
to be a Godsend and a preparation for an intense, six-month-long
period of physical struggle that resulted in that race to the hospital, that prolonged stay there, and major surgery and diagnosis
of an autoimmune disease. In that time, Paul's words regarding
the resurrected and glorified body happened to be the text for

my daily prayers. There was comfort to be found in those words. As I lingered there, though, I found that the answer to my bodily struggles was less interesting than the deeper question. Paul did not await the transformation of his body. Rather, he awaited "the Savior, the Lord Jesus Christ," who happened also to bring with him that subjection of even the death-riddled body. I found that the beauty of Christ, "my beloved," was far more interesting, glorious, and inspiring than even the promise of earthly goods. The example of Paul in this regard—like that of Nyssa and Calvin, of Owen and Lewis—has prompted me to walk in this heavenly minded way. It involves tears, no doubt, but it is not the way of shame. I have found that while I look for the healing of my belly, even that longed-for good is not my god. Setting my mind on earthly things, even when given by God, would be to end in destruction. So, like the martyrs of our day and the apostles of old, I long to "stand firm thus in the Lord." And I remain amazed by those men and women—brothers and sisters around the globe and through the centuries (like the apostle Paul)—who have journeyed in such a way that they demonstrate that they are rejoicing in nothing less than the Lord himself, even when faced with challenges that I can only imagine.

May Christians in the modern West not lose that living hope—the Lord himself and the way of his cross—by being satisfied with lesser goods. May we never forget that we, along with any and all goods that we are given, are ultimately grounded in heaven.

BIBLIOGRAPHIC ESSAY

I have found that the testimony of the early fathers and the later Reformed has been formative in contemplating our living hope. The late Anglican divine Kenneth E. Kirk penned a beautiful volume that drew together the eschatological and the ethical in his *The Vision of God: The Christian Doctrine of the Summum Bonum* (London: Longmans, Green and Co., 1931; repr. New York: Harper & Row, 1966). While I am no Anglo-Catholic, I have found his historical and theological analysis a beneficial point of reference. Ascetical theology and heavenly minded eschatology have not been prominent in recent years, yet I have been aided especially by some notable contrarians. First, I have been provoked by the Augustinian ethics of asceticism and of engagement in Charles Mathewes, *A Theology of Public Life*, Cambridge Studies in Christian Doctrine (Cambridge: Cambridge University Press, 2007). While disagreeing with key judgments regarding intellectual and cultural history and with the specific contours of his proposal for a sacramental metaphysics, I have gleaned from Hans Boersma, *Heavenly Participation: The Weaving of a Sacramental Tapestry* (Grand Rapids: Eerdmans, 2011); and, appreciating her reflections on desire, though with major misgivings regarding elements of her sexual ethics and theology of gender, I have also profited from Sarah Coakley, *The New Asceticism: Sexuality, Gender, and the*

Quest for God (London: Bloomsbury, 2015). I hope that my reflections root these themes more overtly in exegesis of Holy Scripture as well as develop them a bit more systematically in the wider terrain of Christian doctrine. Most significant in this direction, then, have been ways in which the late John Webster began to address ascetical theology from a vantage point rooted in the patristic and medieval tradition's approach to a theological anthropology. He also kept a watchful eye upon the Reformed tradition's concern for remaining vigilant in its commendation of evangelical grace. His soundings in asceticism can be seen especially in later essays now published in *Virtue and Intellect*, vol. 2 of *God without Measure: Working Papers in Christian Theology* (London: T & T Clark, 2015).

All these authors have rooted their reflections in the mind of the church, so I have been led especially to linger over the texts of the patristic and the later Puritan period. The beatific vision and the call to the ascetic life permeated the writings of the church fathers, so one can discover brilliant expositions in often surprising spots. Highly significant analyses can be found in Basil, *Ascetical Works*, trans. Sister Monica Wagner, Fathers of the Church 9 (Washington, DC: Catholic University of America Press, 1962); Gregory of Nyssa, *Ascetical Works*, trans. Virginia Woods Callahan, Fathers of the Church 58 (Washington, DC: Catholic University of America Press, 1967); Gregory of Nyssa, *The Life of Moses*, trans. Abraham Malherbe and Everett Ferguson, Classics of Western Spirituality (New York: Paulist, 1978); and Augustine, *Marriage and Virginity*, ed. John Rotelle, trans. Ray Kearney, Works of Saint Augustine I/9 (Hyde Park, NY: New City, 1999).

Significant work has been done in recent years regarding the exegetical imagination of the ascetical life in a way that shows its parallels to the philosophical life of the Greco-Roman world but also brings out its distinctly Christian elements. Especially helpful here have been the following works: John Behr, *Asceticism and Anthropology in Irenaeus and Clement*, Oxford Early

Christian Studies (Oxford: Oxford University Press, 2000); Elizabeth A. Clark, *Reading Renunciation: Asceticism and Scripture in Early Christianity* (Princeton: Princeton University Press, 1999); Karl Shuve, *The Song of Songs and the Fashioning of Identity in Early Latin Christianity*, Oxford Early Christian Studies (Oxford: Oxford University Press, 2016); Hans Boersma, *Embodiment and Virtue in Gregory of Nyssa: An Anagogical Approach*, Oxford Early Christian Studies (Oxford: Oxford University Press, 2013); Ann Conway-Jones, *Gregory of Nyssa's Tabernacle Imagery in Its Jewish and Christian Contexts*, Oxford Early Christian Studies (Oxford: Oxford University Press, 2014); and Thomas L. Humphries Jr., *Ascetic Pneumatology from John Cassian to Gregory the Great*, Oxford Early Christian Studies (Oxford: Oxford University Press, 2013). Two volumes have helped orient me to the breadth of Augustine's thought here: Oliver O'Donovan's *The Problem of Self-Love in St. Augustine* (New Haven: Yale University Press, 1980; repr. Eugene, OR: Wipf & Stock, 2006); and Matthew Drever, *Image, Identity, and the Forming of the Augustinian Soul*, AAR Academy Series (New York: Oxford University Press, 2013).

My reading of the classical Reformed tradition as well as its developments amongst the Puritans has focused on a few key texts. A new version of Calvin's engagement of ascetical theology has recently been released as John Calvin, *A Little Book on the Christian Life*, ed. Aaron Clay Denlinger and Burk Parsons (Sanford, FL: Reformation Trust, 2017). Without finding their historical arguments about the structure of the *Institutes* or about Calvin's Christology, respectively, convincing, I have nonetheless benefitted from Matthew Myer Boulton, *Life in God: John Calvin, Practical Formation, and the Future of Protestant Theology* (Grand Rapids: Eerdmans, 2011); and from Julie Canlis, *Calvin's Ladder: A Spiritual Theology of Ascent and Ascension* (Grand Rapids: Eerdmans, 2010). John Owen's "The Grace and Duty of Being Spiritually Minded" can be found in William H. Goold, ed., *Sin and Grace*, The Works of John Owen 7 (Edinburgh: Banner of Truth

Trust, 1965). Further reflections can be gained from reading Wilhelmus à Brakel, *The Law, Christian Graces, and the Lord's Prayer*, vol. 3 of *The Christian's Reasonable Service*, ed. Joel Beeke, trans. Bartel Elshout (Grand Rapids: Reformation Heritage, 1994), esp. §56–65.

A metaphysical focus on the spiritual and an eschatological accent on divine communion not only prompt an ethic of heavenly-mindedness but also suggest that the practice of Christian theology ought to involve a commitment to contemplation. I regularly take students through two classic texts of pastoral theology that differ in much but share this fundamental notion that the active life of Christian ministry and soul care stands or falls with an abiding contemplative dimension: Gregory the Great, *The Book of Pastoral Rule*, trans. George Demacopoulos, Popular Patristics 34 (Crestwood, NY: St. Vladimir's Seminary Press, 2007), 58–61, 68–74, 83–85; and Richard Baxter, *The Reformed Pastor*, ed. William Brown (Puritan Paperbacks, 1974), 58–63. Though many in the Reformed world have shied away from the language of contemplation (fearing that it tends toward extra-biblical speculation and/or away from concern for worldly responsibilities), I have sought to develop a Reformed account of the contemplative task of theology by drawing on the work of Thomas Aquinas in "The Active and Contemplative Life: The Practice of Theology," in *Aquinas among the Protestants*, ed. Manfred Svensson and David VanDrunen (Oxford: Blackwell, 2017), 189–206.

INDEX OF AUTHORS

SUBJECT INDEX

SCRIPTURE INDEX